Teaching
Bilingual/Bicultural
Children

Studies in the
Postmodern Theory of Education

Shirley R. Steinberg
General Editor

Vol. 371

PETER LANG
New York • Washington, D.C./Baltimore • Bern
Frankfurt • Berlin • Brussels • Vienna • Oxford

Teaching Bilingual/Bicultural Children

Teachers Talk about Language and Learning

EDITED BY
Lourdes Diaz Soto
and Haroon Kharem

PETER LANG
New York • Washington, D.C./Baltimore • Bern
Frankfurt • Berlin • Brussels • Vienna • Oxford

Library of Congress Cataloging-in-Publication Data
Soto, Lourdes Diaz.
Teaching bilingual/bicultural children: teachers talk about language and learning /
Edited by Lourdes Diaz Soto, Haroon Kharem.
p. cm. — (Counterpoints: Studies in the postmodern theory of education; v.371.)
Includes bibliographical references and index.
1. Education, Bilingual. 2. Multicultural education. 3. Critical pedagogy.
I. Kharem, Haroon. II. Title.
LC3725.S68   370.117—dc22   2010008248
ISBN 978-1-4331-0719-1 (hardcover)
ISBN 978-1-4331-0718-4 (paperback)
ISSN 1058-1634

Bibliographic information published by **Die Deutsche Nationalbibliothek**.
Die Deutsche Nationalbibliothek lists this publication in the "Deutsche
Nationalbibliografie"; detailed bibliographic data is available
on the Internet at http://dnb.d-nb.de/.

Cover photo of children in the doorway of an old school on the
lower east side of Manhattan from the early 1960s courtesy of Omar Kharem

The paper in this book meets the guidelines for permanence and durability
of the Committee on Production Guidelines for Book Longevity
of the Council of Library Resources.

*We would like to dedicate this book
to the bilingual/bicultural children and teachers who struggle in an
often inequitable hegemonic system that looks to deny their culture and language.
Nevertheless,
they continue to overcome obstacles placed in their way with hope in
their hearts filled with dreams and possibilities.*

Table of Contents

Part Two: Critical Analyses: Los Consejos

Foreword

[T]he way we are—the manner in which we eat, what we eat, the way we dress up, the way we behave in the world, how we find ourselves with others and the way we communicate, the levels of education, our class position in the society to which we belong—all these things end up being part of our language, our thinking structure that in turn, conditions us. We experience ourselves in language, we socially create language, and finally we become linguistically competent.[1]

—PAULO FREIRE (1993)

In contemplating the significance of any emancipatory pedagogy that seeks to support the political determination of historically subordinated populations, the key role that language plays in the sociopsychological, intellectual, physical, and spiritual development of the child must remain at the forefront of our theory and practice—for it is truly impossible, as Paulo Freire's opening words suggest, to contemplate our cultural existence outside the realm of language. Even within the womb, the developing babe is bombarded each moment with the sound waves of mother's voice and the echo of family rhythms. The cadence and timbre of intimate conversations and the musical beat of the cultural community all stimulate bodily sensations tied to cultural meaning within the mother and, thus, take root in her child.

Hence, a child's knowledge of language begins long before she or he can clearly enunciate the first recognizable syllable. It is from the inception of life that all organisms, including the human being, are prepared and primed to exist in a world of particular sound formations; sounds which dictate both meaning and a sense of safety and belonging in the world. To use Freire's well-known phrase, we can say that the child actually begins to "read the world" in utero. And as such, any emancipatory bilingual/bicultural pedagogy must fundamentally integrate, in both theory and practice, a fundamental respect for the cultural significance and function of language. This entails a politics of language education that moves far beyond the fragmented, reductive, and instrumentalized views that drive the traditional literacy curriculum and most of what remains as bilingual education in public schools today.

Accordingly, Freire's words also speak to the inextricable relationship that exists between culture and language; a relationship that is firmly punctuated by the power relationships that are at work in the lives of teachers and their students. If culture reflects the manner in which populations have historically survived the conditions in which they exist, then there is no question that language functions as one of the most powerful transmitters of culture and, as such, exists as a powerful mediator of class and racialized inequalities. It is for this reason that cultural values, beliefs, and even disabling myths are often made more apparent by the ways that personal stories are expressed—stories that shed light on the everyday classroom life of bicultural/bilingual teachers. Yet, these important voices, anchored in the real life experiences of those who contend daily with issues of inequality and social exclusions within schools, are the very voices that are so often missing in the discourse of teacher education programs.

With all this clearly in mind, Lourdes Diaz Soto and Haroon Kharem deliberately and conscientiously bring to this volume the voices of bilingual/bicultural educators, in order to engage forthrightly the need for a critical bilingual and bicultural understanding of schooling. In concert with their identities as bilingual/bicultural educators and urban teachers, the contributors to *Teaching Bilingual/Bicultural Children: Teachers Talk about Language and Learning* provide poignant stories with a grounded analysis that sharply differentiates not only their teaching and learning process but the manner in which inequalities within school and society require them to struggle daily with the unexamined complexities of their social location—complexities that are often intensified by the false and stereotypical portrayals of racialized communities in the United States.

A common thread that runs across the book's personal reflections and consejos is the recognition that any effort to bring social justice pedagogy to urban classrooms must contend seriously with what Freire calls "cultural invasion."[2] This phenomenon speaks to the outcome of longstanding oppressive dynamics, in which public schooling has functioned as a deeply colonizing force in the lives of bilingual/bicultural children and their communities. Toward this end, traditional classroom pedagogy and curriculum has been used to systematically strip away the primary cultures and languages of racialized communities, replacing them, instead, with an assimilative "American" identity—a national identity that works to conserve the consolidated power and control of the wealthy and powerful within the nation-state, over those who were historically colonized and enslaved populations.[3]

Given the significant role of the primary language in the development of identity and a sense of belonging, linguistic genocide, as an outcome of cultural invasion, is clearly one of the most devastating consequences faced by bilingual/bicultural students. The negative consequences of placing children in educational contexts that, wittingly or unwittingly, erode their sense of belonging and worthiness set bilingual/bicultural children up to fail academically, despite the fact they enter as capable of learning as their more privileged English-speaking counterparts. The accounts in the book bear witness to the inherently difficult conditions at work in urban schools today. But even more importantly, these stories also illustrate some of the more effective critical practices utilized by educators in supporting bilingual/ bicultural children to retain and enhance connections with their cultural and linguistic roots, despite standardized curricula that masquerade as multicultural fare, traditional pedagogy that projects stereotypical notions of cultural deficit upon bicultural children and their parents, and harsh anti-immigrant sentiments which threaten their sense of safety and security.

Also of key importance to this work is the manner in which the contributors to this volume speak eloquently to the differences that exist between bilingual/bicultural students and within cultural communities—without losing sight of the collective histories and conditions that make bilingual/bicultural children part of distinct cultural and linguistic contexts. Again, this counter-homogenizing skill is very much connected to the past academic struggles faced by these educators, as they too grappled as children to make sense of the often jagged and confusing journeys in constructing bicultural/bicultural identities within a heavily racialized and economically apartheid world. In many ways, their distinct set of pedagogical skills have been developed through the most convincing empirical design—the trial and error of their own suffering and triumphs, first as bilingual/bicultural students and then as teachers of bilingual/bicultural children. Yet, this rich and valuable knowledge has often been ignored or dismissed by traditional educators, who generally hold a limited understanding of worlds outside their monocultural/monolingual existence. For many of these mainstream teachers, to speak of biculturalism generally means little beyond being born outside the U.S., perhaps being non-English-speaking, and/or eating or being "ethnic."

With clear-sightedness toward transforming the ignorance that has plagued teacher preparation programs, Teaching Bilingual/Bicultural Children: Teachers Talk about Language and Learning gathers for our consideration that very knowledge so often deemed illegitimate or inferior or irrelevant or superfluous. Through a variety of personal stories and reflections about the struggle for identity, personal complexities, bilingual/ bicultural teaching practices, and actual classroom examples of social justice pedagogy, the old silences and obstructions are removed and new knowledge unleashed. By so doing, concealed pedagogical wisdom surfaces, so that it can infuse new breath into the teaching and learning of bilingual/bicultural children and revitalize critical principles for a bilingual/bicultural pedagogy.[4] Refreshingly and without apologia, Diaz Soto and Kharem boldly call for a social justice pedagogy that begins with, and builds upon, the cultural and linguistic knowledge of bilingual/bicultural teachers, students, parents, and communities. Anything less rigorous than this will, simply, no longer do.

ANTONIA DARDER
UNIVERSITY OF ILLINOIS AT URBANA-CHAMPAIGN

NOTES

1. Freire, P. (1993). *Pedagogy of the City*. New York: Continuum (p.134).
2. Freire, P. (1971). *Pedagogy of the Oppressed*. New York: Continuum.
3. Darder, A. & Torres, R. D. (2004). *After Race: Racism After Multiculturalism*. New York: NYU Press.
4. For a discussion of the principles of a critical bicultural pedagogy, see Darder, Antonia (1991). *Culture and Power in the Classroom: A Critical Foundation for Bicultural Education*. Westport, CT: Bergin & Garvey.

Introduction

LOURDES DIAZ SOTO & HAROON KHAREM

This edited volume is dedicated to contemporary teachers. Our goal is to provide a practical book for teachers (and pre-service teachers) who work with (or will be working with) bilingual/bicultural children. The authors of these chapters share their personal wisdom garnered from working in classrooms with bilingual/bicultural learners. The pieces present the insider's perspective since each educator is herself/himself bilingual/bicultural. The narrative chapters we have collected serve to highlight experiences teachers and scholars would like to share with you about best practices and possibilities for teaching bilingual/bicultural children.

This book provides practical knowledge for teachers who are struggling to meet the needs of increasingly diverse classrooms. We have chosen to highlight two themes: the first theme relies on personal reflections from the contributors while the second portion focuses on a critical analysis of the complexities involved in our contemporary classrooms.

The themes you will read about divide the book into two sections:

I   Personal Reflections
II Critical Analyses

The first section of the book depicts how our contributors reflect on their own lives as both teachers of bilingual/bicultural learners and as bilingual/bicultural subjects themselves. The following descriptions highlight the first section: Charise Pimentel relates in Chapter 2 her experience as a woman who is stereotyped as a "Barbie" in spite of the complexity of her bilingual/bicultural experience. In Chapter 3 Linda Jackson, Sheila Guzman, and Guadalupe Ramos, three Mexican American teachers, share their journey that includes the importance of "la educacion" and the value of cultural identity for teachers. In Chapter 4 Alma Rubal-Lopez amplifies the great advantages of being bilingual and depicts the complexities of the Nuyorican experience. In Chapter 5 Luis Urrieta reflects on additional complexities revealing why some parents may feel that bilingual education is not for them. María R. Scharrón-del Río, Chapter 6, shares the richness of intergenerational storytelling and gives us a glimpse of her experience as a Puerto Rican scholar/counselor in New York City.

The second part of the book provides critical analyses of programs and practices while offering consejos (advice) for the teachers engaged in the pedagogical struggle. In Chapter 7 Delida Sanchez focuses on how race matters to her and the children she teaches. In Chapter 8 Octavio Pimentel depicts the complexities of the bicultural/bilingual experience for his son and for himself since they do not fit the stereotypical models. In Chapter 9 Frances Rains situates herself and then shares the powerful voices of American Indian parents. In Chapter 10 Marion Neville Lynch focuses on teacher beliefs while describing the implications of rigid testing mandates. In Chapter 12 Noelle Gentile describes the value of social action-education projects in the aftermath of Hurricane Katrina. Elizabeth Quintero, in Chapter 15, shares the power of students' and teachers' personal stories. In her Chapter 16 Irene Garza relates the immigration journey for children growing up in Texas as well as the role of the Bracero project. Finally, in Chapter 17 Haroon Kharem and Genevieve Collura provide ways teachers can rethink pedagogical attitudes in the bicultural/bilingual classroom.

WHY IS THIS BOOK NEEDED?

If the main task of a teacher is to provide students the opportunity to learn, then it is imperative that teachers gain the needed specialized knowledge about the challenges faced by bicultural/bilingual teachers and children in our public school system.

Professors Kharem and Soto share common urban childhoods. In spite of our differing personal historical and sociocultural contexts, these shared experiences have helped us to gain insights about the complexities currently evidenced in urban classrooms. Our experiences as children, parents, grandparents, teachers, researchers, and student-teacher supervisors have added additional layers of understanding to the struggles teachers face on a daily basis.

Our personal experiences are the starting points and have been in the forefront of our narrative inquiry. Instead of abstract empirical queries we decided to move ahead with this project through a continual position of experience that is accumulated, analyzed and interpreted by the authors. Teachers are attempting to teach under often difficult circumstances from policy makers and administrators, in dilapidated buildings with scant resources. This edited volume reveals the layers of complexities as it provides the needed teacher-contemporary voices for both existing and future teachers.

Personal Reflections

Mi Vida Como Maestra

Engaging the World of Teacher Preparation on Behalf of Bilingual/Bicultural Learners

LOURDES DIAZ SOTO & HAROON KHAREM

Preparing teacher candidates in an urban context is not only rigorous but also a sensitive journey into the lives of future teachers as well as the lives of the students. The need for a "rigorous and just urban pedagogy" supports the fact that each school is different and that it is imperative that potential teachers study the community that surrounds each individual school. In order to bring a "rigorous and just urban pedagogy" into the classroom, it should be a requisite that teacher candidates examine the socioeconomics and cultural capital of the community they intend to serve. There must be an analysis of the positions of empowerment as well as the point of disempowerment of the students and their community. This type of research and participation will encourage teacher candidates to choose whether they will become community teachers or outsiders collecting a pay check. Like medical interns, teacher candidates are placed in schools to gain valuable experience about the children they are going to teach and about the communities they are going to serve. Most schools of education prepare teacher candidates from a positivist paradigm that separates feelings from facts, that bases its finding upon empirical objective data alone and eschews any emotional involvement (Ladson-Billings, 2001; Murrell, 2001; Steinberg & Kincheloe, 2004).

Jacqueline Jordan Irvine (2003) emphasizes that many teacher candidates are not prepared to teach diverse student populations. Instructors/professors cannot allocate just a few minutes or one session within their course syllabi to diverse populations and expect teacher candidates to be socially just, prepare culturally relevant curricula, and/or be allied with the community they serve. Nor can college professors/instructors expect to prepare teacher candidates on issues of diversity when they are not knowledgeable and experienced in diverse populations. Geneva Gay (2000) affirms this notion when she asserts that those who believe that "good teachers anywhere are good teachers everywhere...fail to realize that their standard of goodness is culturally determined and is not the same for all ethnic groups" (p. 22).

It is not uncommon for a teacher to have students from several Spanish speaking countries in low-income communities or to have students from East Asia or the African Diaspora speaking different languages and possessing different cultural norms all in one class. For example, we have observed schools that not only have a diversity of Spanish speaking students but also students that are African American, African, Caribbean, all of African descent, all culturally different, and all with different language dialects. Furthermore, families from countries like Pakistan and (including families from traditionally Muslim regions of the world) are moving into low-income urban communities and send their children to schools with populations consisting mainly of segregated Black and Latino students. All these diverse ethnic groups are trying to learn together in hard-to-staff schools, taught by teachers who are not culturally prepared to teach such a diverse group (Sunshine & Warner, 1998).

How can we prepare teachers to teach in such aforementioned classrooms with all the ethnic diversity in one college or professional development class session? There is an abundance of literature on teaching diverse populations by respected researchers, yet very little of it is reaching college teacher preparation programs. This is important, especially for students attending segregated, hard-to-staff schools that employ alternate route teachers who may not meet basic certification standards.

Rigorous preparation of teacher candidates within an urban context entails more than objective theoretical frameworks. Teacher preparation also includes the subjective intuitive knowledge far beyond any empirical studies that can only come from a knowledge that is not just textbook learning but from being immersed in the community whose children we are teaching. This intuitive knowledge assists the teacher in solving problems and supporting students to become successful citizens far beyond any data can achieve. The empirical data can help support a teacher's decision but not control the process of decision-making. This process includes the need to understand the exclusion and marginalization of non white people, the poor, women and the consideration of their daily-lived realities.

Teacher candidates can also be prepared to comprehend the historical complexities of the groups they are teaching and have a working knowledge of what it means to struggle and to achieve in the midst of obstacles that seem overwhelming. In many schools of education, little thought is given to the knowledge that would address the history and culture of bilingual/bicultural students and their struggles to survive and be successful in a society that consistently excludes and marginalizes their lives.

The Complexities of Bilingual/Bicultural Sociocultural Contexts

Issues of language and culture continue to impact how schools and our nation view both learners and learning. The idea that language is the carrier of perceptions, attitudes and goals is certainly evidenced in our contemporary realities. Scholars have struggled with how language issues can ultimately be an integral part of power issues. Pennycook (1998), for example, describes how English around the world is not only at the "heart of colonialism" but is also deeply interwoven with the discourses of colonialism. He notes how language can bestow civilization, knowledge, and wealth while at the same time being racially defined.

Macias (1996) documents the return of open hostility toward non white and immigrant learners by the majority population. Language (and culture) continues to be a site of struggle in the "post colonial ." We see the need to bracket "post colonial" since for diverse "others," for the indigenous peoples, workers, women of color, non-white and Americans on the hyphen, the poor the colonial is very much with us at the macro-sociopolitical level, at the grassroots community level, as well as within our daily-lived realities.

Macedo (2000) notes the irony of how America has dismantled bilingual education, a field with decades of research, while promoting foreign language education, a field with well-documented failures. Whites who fear that America will lose its Anglo-Protestant cultural roots have eliminated the very programs that can help our children and our nation (Soto, 1997).

Language is important because it can either enhance a child's education or destroy a child's progress in school and leave the child to languish on the margins of society. Schools have even gone so far as to forbid children from speaking their own language altogether (Stubbs, 2002).

Timothy Reagan (2002) argues:

> Effective, meaningful education is possible only when we recognize the fundamentally political and ideological nature of schooling. Education is not, cannot, and should not be apolitical. This does not mean that indoctrination is acceptable; indeed, only by helping students recognize the political and ideological underpinnings of contemporary social and educational institutions can we prepare them to make their own informed political decisions. This, I believe, should be one of the central goals of all schooling in a democratic society (p. x).

We have noted that so often the ivory tower, and its accompanying scholarship, labels the majority of non white student population as "at risk," or describes schools attended by predominately Black and Latino children as "high-need or hard-to-staff" schools. Has anyone asked the children labeled "at risk or deficit model learners" what he or she thinks of being called and labeled a pathologic social disease? What African American or Latino walks around calling him or herself "at risk" or "underclass?" (These acronyms are used as evasive measures so that the dominant culture does not have to confront the issue of race and class.)

Macedo and Bartolomé (1999) use the term "shock words" to describe how the middle class is used against the poor and non white groups of people (p. 23). This insidious ideology is used to resist bilingual/bicultural education, programs that can benefit and help assist in educating children. Another shock term is "culturally deprived" a term defined as lacking the cultural morals of the dominant Anglo-Protestant society. These shock words are powerful and they are used to make the targeted victims appear sickly, in need of medical attention and/or in need of a moral education—teaching them the morals and values of the dominant group. Thus, schooling becomes a powerful ideological tool to indoctrinate children with the value systems and language of their oppressor.

Language also classifies people. It is an "indication of class and cultural background" and if not used correctly it makes you inferior to the dominant group. Teachers correct and discourage children from speaking or writing in their home language, and if teachers are not careful they end up silencing the child thus causing more harm than good (Christensen, 1995).

In addition, language becomes a powerful tool to make nonwhites invisible, allowing the dominant culture to call for a color-blind society that claims to not see race in the classroom, thus strengthening the dominant White culture. This color-blind ideology forces nonwhites to assimilate into the dominant culture; blaming the victims of racism while absolving teachers of the responsibility of confronting racism, power and discrimination in the classroom (Revilla, Wells, & Holme, 2004; Schofield, 1997).

The English language thus becomes oppressive as it builds a bulwark to keep people out. Yet it incorporates those who master it enough to serve the colonizer's needs and only values the "native language" when being entertained. Therefore, the colonizer can "weigh the colonizer's language, history, and community experiences and then decide that the value is nil."

In other words the subjugated must wear the "white mask" to be successful in the colonizer's world (Dowdy, 2002, p. 11).

CONSIDERING ISSUES OF POWER

Children are systematically stripped of their integrity, independence, freedom, and voice in this form of linguistic colonization. This is a form of educational violence and slaying the soul that serves to perpetrate social control and seeks to keep the colonized as little children who are in need of civilization. Children are denied their ability to participate in school and community life because their voices are silenced and they are unable to enter into dialogue unable to reflect on their daily realities and lived experiences. Ultimately this marginalization leads to multiple and complex issues for children, including issues of identity and biliteracy (Constantino, 1978).

As the privileged assert their superiority, bicultural children continue to lead an oppressed existence while continually reaching out to the "other" with love and compassion. "To live in the Borderlands means you are neither hispana india negra espanola ni gabachacha, eres mestiza, mulata, half-breed while carrying all five races on your back not knowing which side to turn to, run from" (Anzaldúa, 1999, p. 216; Soto, 2002b).

Joshua Fishman, noting that 1.6 billion people, nearly one third of the world's population, will use English in some form, asks, "Is English the killer language?" Fishman examines the debate on whether the spread represents benign globalization or a form of linguistic imperialism. This well-respected linguist has reasons to believe that the English language will eventually wane in influence. There is no reason to believe that English will always be necessary for technology, higher education, and social mobility since "ultimately democracy, international trade and economic development can flourish in any tongue" (Fishman, 1998, 2000).

Fishman's question "is English the killer language?" leads us to examine the possibility that the influence of English will diminish with the increased growth in local/regional relations. The spread of regional languages occurs with the advent of local/regional communications, informal social interactions/networks, interethnic families, travel, worship, exchange of goods, and migration. Issues of identity are also fostered with their symbolic functions and a call for authentic cultural markers.

The complexities faced by our nation, along with the changing demographics within the U. S. public schools, point to the need for preparing teachers with the knowledge and competencies for working with the rapidly increasing population of students from diverse backgrounds. Zeichner and Hoeft underscore the urgency of this matter in their extensive review of the literature in teacher education. They document how teachers in the United States, who are primarily White, middle-class, monolingual (unlike their students) with limited experiences of diverse groups, perceive diversity with negative connotations (Zeichner & Hoeft, 1996)

VALUING CLASSROOM TEACHERS' VOICES

The power of teachers' voices lies in the fact that they are the experts on what is happening in classrooms. Teachers' voices, so often disregarded in discussions on education, can provide the wisdom, the knowledge and the needed directions for the field, for other teachers and for novice teachers. Much of the existing education literature and teacher education course-work instructs teachers about methodology (what they should do) without asking them about their own experiences. Rarely are teachers asked what they really think about their individual pedagogical practices; what they do and need; or about the realities of their work with students. In addition, policy makers do not ask teachers about the effects of the policies and curricula forced upon them by federal, state, district, and school mandates.

Connolly and Clandinin refer to teacher narratives as both a phenomenon and a method of inquiry. As a phenomenon, narratives are the stories themselves, which characterize the values and experience of teachers. As a method of inquiry, the voices of teachers become the primary focus of research in teacher education and its potential to articulate to practitioners and correctly represent the value of teaching. These "first and secondhand accounts of individuals, teachers, students, classrooms, written by teachers and others" (p. 4) not only bring new ideas to research but also consistently represent the value of the intuitive experience of teachers and their craft. They can capture the wealth and array of teachers' knowledge and actions and describe the complexity of teaching. As such, the stories and narratives of teachers "have the power to direct and change our lives" (Connelly & Clandinin, 1990; Noddings, 1991, cited in Carter, 1993).

The value of teachers' voices also lies in allowing the reader to vicariously walk in another's shoes and experience other ideas and other points of view. We see a need to highlight the voices of bilingual/bicultural teachers, who teach, by association with language and culture, children that have been marginalized in school and society. Reading the stories of teachers' expertise in diverse situations brings insight into the actions that form their professional knowledge. Reflecting collaboratively on the stories and their lessons can provide an understanding of how teachers make sense of their experiences and incorporate them into their personal practical knowledge (Macedo & Bartolomé 1999; Montero-Sieburth & Perez, 1987; Richardson, 1994).

When we value teachers' voices we learn that each teacher brings unique experiences and strengths, not as a miracle worker but within the realistic complexities coupled with the rewards of the classroom experiences. Sharing stories and lessons among teachers can build a sense of community, reduce isolation so prevalent in teaching, and encourage teachers to see themselves as intentional practitioners integrating expertise and intuitive knowledge into their practice. All of these factors combine to assist teachers in recognizing and facilitating change in their professional lives. They are no longer institutional machines but human beings who fail, get frustrated, at times depressed yet willing to start each new day with the hope of reaching the most challenging children and succeeding. Teachers use their narratives to counteract their own and their students' marginalization, and their struggles to teach effectively and gain acceptance within the contexts of their particular schools.

There is another aspect to the narrative that brings to life the teacher's experience and involvement within the community he/she teaches. Peter Murrell argues that teachers and teacher candidates in professional development programs become community teachers by drawing upon the local knowledge, perspectives, and cultural frameworks of the neighborhood they serve. In other words, teachers must become participants in the objectives that the community surrounding the school sets out to accomplish and develop a genuine understanding of the cultural values of the local community. While many non-white teachers are in ideological congruence with Murrell's findings, many educators and those who make policy rarely take his framework on community teaching seriously. Some would rather stay at a distance and depend solely upon empirical quantitative data without ever venturing into the communities they are hired to serve (Murrell, 2001).

Murrell's community teaching falls in line with Ming Fang He (2008) research that highlights how the traditional empirical ways of interpreting research are being called into question by personal, passionate, and participatory action research. This qualitative critical framework aims to develop a different method to examine issues of diversity and social justice in education. This can be done by concentrating on understanding the numerous intricate dimensions of the experience of individuals, families, and communities who are misrepresented and marginalized in research. Instead of detached and abstract quantitative research (where the data may not closely reflect such marginalized student populations), personal, and passionate, participatory inquiry arises from the experience of researchers and participants. This method analyzes personal field records, autobiographical documents, and narratives as the starting point of inquiry. Such methods allow teachers to become fluid rather than fixed points as the lives of students and communities change. Teachers can seek permission and become a part of the local community, build personal relationships rather than remain detached observers that Linda Tuhiwai Smith talks about in *Decolonizing Methodologies* (1999).

THE COMPLEXITIES OF TEACHER EDUCATION

The need to enhance teacher education is crucial as we note that America's schools are failing our children. The National Center for Education Statistics (NCES) notes that learners living in families with incomes in the lowest 20% were five times more likely to drop out of high school. They also noted that Latino students are more likely than other groups to drop out of high school. The NCES in 2005, showed that Latino/a dropout rates still exceed those of Whites and Blacks. More important-ly, the latest NCES report states that one out of four Latinos between the ages of 16 and 24 drop out of high school. Gonzalez Juenke indicates that the Latino dropout rate is twice that of Whites and significantly higher than that of African Americans. As we view these figures, NCES notes that public elementary and sec-ondary enrollment is projected to increase to 50 million by the year 2014. These fig-ures help to make the case that we need to enhance existing and future teacher knowledge so they can in turn provide appropriate and responsive expertise (Juenke 2004; Laird et al., 2007).

Paulo Freire has long taught us that teaching is not a paternalistic coddling pro-fession but that it requires constant intellectual rigor and a curiosity for knowledge. He also argues that teachers are not tools for psychometric statistical data; instead teachers can guide students to question, explore, and voice their human right to fight for the intellectual freedom to express their own opinions. Freire further asserts that teachers can incite their students to create their own knowledge of an object or topic and that teaching is a two-way street where teachers and students freely exchange ideas back and forth.

Teachers have one of the greatest responsibilities and one of the hardest jobs of any profession. They are entrusted with the lives of other people's children to pro-duce the next generation of civic-minded citizens. Teachers can experience exhaus-tion and burn out while working in low-income communities where racism and historical discriminatory practices have been upheld. In addition, teachers struggle when preparing students amidst federal mandates that hurt students and teachers more than they help. Teacher turnover rate is high because of all these factors as well as in addition to scripted curricula that discourage teacher creativity (Johnson, Berg, & Donaldson, 2005).

Teaching is giving of one's inner self and makes the teacher transparent in the eyes of the students. Students can see through teachers, they can discern between those who really care to educate and those who teach from a deficit model. Students have a way of bringing out biases within teachers that inform our teaching, influ-ence classroom interaction, and expose how our own belief system may impact the grades and lives of certain students. This is important because our biases can inflict pain upon students; it will cause us to label students as at risk (Ayers & Ford, 1996, p. 4).

One time I (Professor Kharem) was talking to a teacher whose back was toward me. She said, "I wish these kids had the ability to learn." When she turned around to face me, she realized what she had said and was embarrassed. Her racial bias affected how she viewed her students and in turn influenced her pedagogy. It also raised questions: Why was she teaching in a school of predominately African and

Latino American children? How did her racism influence her perception of her students, how she taught, and the grades she assigned students?

It is important for teachers to understand their own perceptions. When teachers critically analyze their own racial biases they begin to uncover new possibilities. We know teaching is difficult and we see the evidence of burnout from multiple requirements including mandated bureaucratic paperwork, meetings, and long hours of preparation. However, if an educator is unable to demonstrate positive engagement in his/her pedagogy, then this person is only perpetuating psychological violence to themselves and to their students. When hopelessness sets in, it is then that a teacher needs the strength and narratives of their peers and mentors to help heal their own internal damage.

We do not believe that all teachers want to inflict their own pain and hurt on their students but if teaching comes from inside us, as Parker J. Palmer suggests, then when one is teaching in the midst of hurt and pain, the hurt and pain will also come out, inflict pain and hurt students. The experience of the teachers' hurt and pain can be used after a time of healing as a base to encourage and strengthen students in their own time of need. In many schools today thousands of students are hurting and in pain, looking for that one understanding soul to identify with them in their time of unrest and turmoil. It is here where teachers can listen to the stories and narratives of other teachers to gain the strength or realize all they do is not in vain. When I (Professor Kharem) teach graduate courses filled with practicing teachers, some of my best teaching has taken place when I taught from my heart and the experiences I encountered and survived from my childhood and adulthood. It was through my own personal narratives of my life that I was able to touch and see the spark in the eyes of my students. Sometimes teacher narratives and stories can reach others more than a text (Palmer, 1998).

Starting in the 1970s, the United States began testing students to assess performance and with the publication of *A Nation at Risk* (National Commission on Excellence in Education, 1983), standardized testing became the principal means to judge the performance of students and teachers. Underlining this publication is the quest for global military and economic dominance supported by politicians catering to corporate leaders and other interest groups are responsible for spiraling "test scores into a symbol of government achievement." Today in our data-driven society teachers are forced to teach to the test, forced to maintain a certain type of classroom management that makes students into robotic beings who regurgitate selected information back to the teacher under the guise of critical thinking. Dedicated, progressive teachers have had to adjust and change their tactics in order to continue teaching and give instruction that leads to student success (Natriello & Pallas, 2001; Spring, 2005, p. 1).

Today, technology and data-driven test scores have replaced teacher knowledge as the barometer of student achievement. Teachers are now told to teach from pre-scribed curricula, forced to use test prep courses that cost schools billions every year, rely upon scores to assess students and leave their own individual judgment and intu-ition at home. Nevertheless, teachers that use their skills to be creative still rely upon their intuition and knowledge, bypass technology and test scores to bring about suc-cess in their classrooms. As more and more teachers respect their craft, reflect upon their practices and experiences, students are able to do well. In some schools, new teachers are left to themselves until the principal observes them; teaching quick-ly becomes a survival of the fittest and the art of teaching develops into complet-ing prepackaged lessons that become drudgery. However, the progressive teachers see their vocation not just as a job but as a craft, a skill that forces one into a con-tinuum of learning. These teachers' reflective practices become narratives with each other and themselves, critically analyzing and asking questions such as: What led them into teaching? What role do they play in the success of students? Where is the profession of teaching leading them? How do they define good teaching? What are the disappointments and how do they deal with losing hope? These are just some of the possible questions that can engage teachers in their own consci-entization (consciousness raising). In What Keeps Teachers Going? Sonia Nieto convincingly argues that "good teaching can overcome difficult handicaps such as poverty or other social ills…there is growing research that good teachers make the single greatest difference in promoting or discouraging student achievement" (p. 2). While scores provide some idea of assessment, it is the intuitive, reflective skill and craft of teaching that weighs heavily upon student achievement (Nieto, 2003).

Some believe that if they take a certain class at a college or attend a conference, they will find the right formula to bringing success in the classroom. Afterward, many teachers are still unfulfilled and more frustrated, while others have learned to see that college classrooms and conferences are only facilitators for teachers to glean from one another. Teachers provide the best learning tools for each other when they reflect and tell their stories among themselves. While academic research is valid and a source of learning, nothing can replace the experience of teachers, their despair, disappointments, victories or success. Teachers who share their classroom practices with other teachers reflect and see that their experience is not in a vacu-um nor are they alone in their struggle to bring about success in their classrooms. They are able to see the resourcefulness of other teachers who sacrifice themselves, take professional and personal risks to make the educational system work to the advantage of neglected marginalized and hurt students. Many outside the circles of teachers never see the inner strength of teachers and their power to change the lives of children in a profound way. Teachers know that students who challenge them con-stantly, students who give them a hard time in class, come back the next year to hug the teacher who did not give up on them.

Teachers carry a wealth of information inside them and spend a lot of time reflecting on their hopes, agonies, attitudes; they plan, revise, analyze, learn and construct stories about their classrooms when they interact with others. The stories in turn become mirrors of their lives, they reflect, learn more about who they are when examining the attitudes, actions and insights of their fellow teachers. Good teachers learn not to stereotype students, they reflect with one another about the conditions of their students and refuse to allow their classrooms to become slave plantations where students always plot to find a way to escape from the classroom. Palmer says a good teacher realizes that the "Student from Hell" is not born in Hell but is "created by conditions beyond his or her control" (p. 45). This reminds me of the little third grade boy who was being reprimanded for behavior problems in front of the principal, assistant principal, his teacher, his mother's boyfriend, others walking along in the hallway, and me. After the child was led away, the assistant principal told me the boy was living with his grandmother who was not able to care for him or his siblings, which placed the responsibility of caretaker on him. I asked the question: Why isn't anyone taking his home situation into account for his behavior? Can't you see his behavior is a call for help? The assistant principal's response was one of disdain; she said, "his behavior is no excuse; he just needs to learn to listen."

Good teachers are great listeners; they can see that a student's arrogance could be just a mask, hiding their fear that they cannot read or some other outside circumstance, and seek a deeper understanding of a student's life. Empirical knowledge demands that teachers be objective and detached from the lives of their students, but good teachers are subjective and very involved in the lives of their students, they form communities in their classrooms. They teach to create spaces for their students to be themselves, to express who they are inside, and build a fortress of trust within the classroom. Their narratives provide sparks that grow into fires in the lives of their peers, they provide access in linking teachers where they are, have been, and where they are going in their career. Narratives also throw light into their pedagogical style whether it is negative or positive. They can stimulate one to reconceptualize curriculum, thereby reaching students previously uninterested. Teachers who work together in the same school and/or grade level can share narratives with one another about a particular student and together take positive action to help the student to progress.

CONCLUSION

In order for our educational programs to move beyond existing models our learners need to be able to read the word and the world bilingually, biculturally, and multiculturally. In the post-monolingual society that we envision, *Teaching*

Bilingual/Bicultural Children: Teachers Talk about Language and Learning, a "critical bilingual/bicultural education" will ensure rigorous learning along with biliteracy, biculturalism and the opportunity for human dignity with democratic participation. How might we heal and end the madness without trying to be saviors? Students are not looking for someone to come in and rescue them from alleged broken homes or uncaring parents. Students are looking for teachers who care and "keep it real," teachers who are willing to listen and accept a student's version of a particular topic. As we move beyond the binaries of power in solidarity toward critically biliterate and multi-literate communities of compassion, it may be that our sisters of color, minorities on the hyphen, monolingual Americans, and the poor and disenfranchised may begin to experience elements of decolonization and liberation. Schools need teachers who are not only looking to pick up a paycheck but who are committed to providing quality education in spite of all the struggles and difficult circumstances their students endure every day. The narratives of teachers can provide insight into the oppressive nature their students resist and struggle to not give up. A retired teacher once told me that "the very fact kids come to this school building tells us they want to learn!" Together, as educators, as allies, as learners, as teachers, we can explore spaces of healing for our common wisdom, our common good, and our love for each other.

CHAPTER TWO

Color-coded Bilingualism

CHARISE PIMENTEL

Tall, blonde hair, and blue eyes—some may even say I resemble Barbie—if I were thinner and better looking. While my appearance may resemble a rough image of Barbie, my lived experiences more closely resemble those of Maria la del Barrio. I grew up around Mexicanos (recent Mexican immigrants who were strongly grounded in the Mexican culture and the Spanish language) in a small migrant community in Northern California. As a result of growing up in this environment, I developed a bilingual and bicultural identity. In my hometown I am referred to as "La güera" (an informal term of endearment for a light-complected person) or "Chavela" (the name of a famous actress, which was easier to pronounce because my name "Charise" contains the sound "Sh" that is not part of the Spanish language). I grew up enjoying, and currently still enjoy, chilaquiles, menudo, y tacos de tripas much more than a meal from Denny's. I feel more comfortable speaking Spanish than English, although I still speak Spanish with an English accent. The reality is, I feel more comfortable among brown people than White people. When my Chicano husband and I decided to have children, we made a commitment to raise our children in a Mexicano, Spanish-speaking household. This commitment has meant that we speak to our children in Spanish only.

Speaking Spanish to my children at home has gone relatively smoothly and uninterrupted. Speaking Spanish to my children in public places, however, has produced many awkward moments, in which people stop, listen, and then proceed to comment and/or ask a number of questions. Some of these comments and questions include, "You speak Spanish very well!," "Where are you from?," "What language are you speaking?," "Why are you teaching Spanish to your children?," "How is it that you learned Spanish?," and "Where did you learn Spanish?" etc. The ongoing questions that I receive, nearly on a daily basis, demonstrate that my bilingualism, as understood in relation to my racial identity, is a novelty. More than that, the fact that I speak Spanish presents incongruence between my racial and linguistic identities. The purpose of this chapter is to examine the intersections of race and language from my experiences as a White, bilingual, academic, mother of Mexicano children. I analyze the concept of "race" because I am looking at how language expectations are informed by discourses that draw from and give meaning to the socially constructed categories that people have created based on physical characteristics. These racial discourses which give rise to language expectations include: (1) White Americans are not bilingual, (2) languages are color-coded, and (3) bilingualism is a foreign language practice (learned while in another country).

These discourses are not surprising given the history of language practices in the United States and more specifically the history of bilingual education. Baker (2006) explains that it is a popular yet misconceived notion that bilingual education serves as a barrier to students' academic success by prohibiting students from learning English, from acculturating into White American culture, and causing cognitive confusion. As a result of these misperceptions, bilingual education has a long history of being discouraged, if not outright denied, in U.S. schools. Even now, most language minority students are placed in remedial language programs, including English as a Second Language (ESL), English Immersion, and Transitional Bilingual Education (TBE) programs, all of which center on the goal of learning English to the detriment of students' native languages (Collier, Thomas, & Tinajero, 2006; Hill, Gómez, & Gómez, 2008). As a result of these language practices in schools, bilingualism is usually a product of language practices produced in the home and/or from schooling in another country. Sadly, most native languages are lost by the third generation of being in the United States (Chacón & Davis, 2006).

Moreover, native English-speaking children, many of whom are White, have historically been excluded from bilingual education altogether. Aside from the relatively new implementations of dual language programs in the United States, native English-speaking students usually do not have the opportunity to take classes to learn a second language until high school when it is offered as a foreign language. Even after they have taken a few foreign language classes in high school or college, native English-speakers' fluency in the second language is often superficial (Baker, 2006; Meiden, 1958). Baker (2006) states:

> In the US and Britain, despite extensive foreign language learning in school (and the extensive research on second language acquisition), only a small proportion of children learning

a foreign language become functionally and fluently bilingual. In the US, fewer than one in 20 children become bilingual following foreign language instruction (p. 120).

Given the inadequacy of foreign language instruction and the overwhelming monolingual English language instruction that native English-speakers are offered in schools, it is difficult to conceive that native English-speakers, again, many of whom are White, are anything but monolingual. Considering the push for monolingualism, and more specifically English, only in our schools and government, we can better understand how my bilingualism, as well as my children's Spanish monolingualism, does not fit into observers' racially informed language expectations. In the following sections, I share three narratives from my experiences in public spaces that demonstrate how observers make sense of me and my children's language practices.

DAME LA LECHE

As stated previously, I do not speak any English to my children, so when we go to a public place like a grocery store, all of my verbal communication with them is in Spanish. Needless to say, taking three young children (no toquen la comida; Sientate bien en el carrito; Qué clase de comidas les gustarían para la casa; ¡Dulce no!; Tienen que estar caminando aqui conmigo, etc.). As I go through the aisles of a grocery store, many people stop and listen, not knowing how to respond. Others observe and then ask questions. A White woman at a local grocery store initiated the following dialogue when I asked my daughter to grab a gallon of milk and put it into our cart.

Charise:	¿Quetzalli, me puedes agarrar un galón de leche del refrigerador y ponerlo en el carrito?
Quetzalli:	¿Cuál mami, la de la tapadera azul o roja?
Charise:	Roja.
Woman:	Oh wow! Are you speaking German to her?
Charise:	No. It's Spanish.
Woman:	Oh, you must be from Spain!

In this dialogue, it becomes clear that all three of the racial discourses I have identified, namely (1) White Americans are not bilingual, (2) languages are color-coded, and (3) bilingualism is a foreign language practice (learned while in another country), shape the language expectations voiced by this woman in the grocery store. The first discourse I have identified, White Americans are not bilingual, shapes how this woman responds to my language practices. The woman assumes I speak English because she speaks to me in English. She also knows that I speak another language, unidentifiable to her, so she realizes that I am bilingual. She then proceeds to make sense of my bilingualism in relation to me and my children's White racial identity. Informed by the dominant discourse that White Americans are not bilingual, she proceeds to designate our language practices as foreign—originating from another country (employing the third discourse). Given our racial identity information, it is not just any language or country that she identifies. Rather, languages are color-coded (the second discourse), so Spanish, the language she observed us speaking, is designated as a minority and inferior language spoken by racial others from Latin America. Because our racial make-up does not register as minority, she configures us as European bilinguals. She first asks if we are speaking German, and when I clarify that it is Spanish we are speaking, our race continues to guide how she makes sense of my bilingualism, so she locates our ability to speak Spanish as originating from Spain. In this example, it becomes clear that languages, as well as bilingualism, are color-coded, whereby language practices are comprehended in conjunction with one's racial identity.

¡Están en la Clase Equivocada!

In this narrative I do not speak at all. However the context in which my son and I are situated, a bilingual classroom, in conjunction with our racial identities, produces an assumption that we are misplaced. This narrative begins on a morning when I dropped off my son at school where he was attending a bilingual pre-K program. Upon entering the room, my son, Quetzin, did not pay much attention to the fact that his usual teacher, Señora Vasquez, was absent and that there was a substitute in her place. As Quetzin customarily does, he proceeded to pull his homework out of his backpack, place it on the front table near the door of the room, hang his backpack on the back wall, and give me a kiss goodbye. Despite my son's actions to settle into the classroom, all signaling that he was right where he needed to be, the substitute teacher stopped me on my way out of the room to say, "I'm sorry ma'am, I think you are in the wrong classroom." Knowing that she was making inferences based on race, I replied to her in Spanish, "Ahora no está Señora Vasquez?" And then she replied in Spanish, "Oh, Perdóneme! No. Fue al doctor ahora."

Because my son and I did not speak at all, the only information available to the substitute teacher that day was our perceived race, and as the above narrative indicates, that was enough to make inferences about the language(s) we spoke. The discourses, White Americans are not bilingual, along with languages are color-coded, came into play in the substitute teacher's interpretation of White people in a bilingual classroom. That is, our White racial identity cued her expectations of our language status: monolingual English-speakers. The discourse that tells us that White Americans are not bilingual led her to believe that neither my son nor I were bilingual and thus we were misplaced in a bilingual classroom. In reality, by drawing from the discourse that White Americans are not bilingual, the teacher only misdiagnosed my language identity, because I am indeed bilingual. My son, however, is not bilingual. Consequently, the discourse that White Americans are not bilingual does not work in contradiction to his language practices. This is where the discourse "languages are color-coded" comes into play. So even if my son was accurately perceived as a monolingual, it was not assumed he was a Spanish-speaking monolingual, thus his misplacement in the classroom. Rather, his racial identity color-coded the language expectation: English-speaking monolingual. With these racially informed language expectations, the teacher thought she could be helpful by telling us that we were in the wrong place, a place designated for bilinguals and/or Spanish monolinguals only.

No Puedes Tomar el Autobús

In the following narrative, in which I was told my son was not qualified to use the school bus, I continue to illustrate how racial discourses (White Americans are not bilingual and languages are color-coded) inform language expectations. This narrative occurred on my son's first day of Kindergarten in a dual language program in Spanish and English. At the end of Quetzin's first day of school, I waited patiently at home for his bus to drop him off. His bus arrival time went by and I continued to wait patiently, realizing that the buses take longer than usual on the first day of school. I waited another half an hour before I called the school to confirm with the teacher that he was indeed put on the right bus. Assured that he was on the right bus, I continued to wait another half an hour before I called the school district to ask them to call the bus driver to check on Quetzin's whereabouts. The school district told me they would call the bus driver and then call me back with Quetzin's status. Twenty more minutes went by before I received a call from the district telling me that Quetzin would be dropped off at the transportation building and that I need to go pick him up. Quetzin was on the bus for two hours by the time he arrived at the transportation office.

This situation was very frustrating to me because I called the transportation office a week before Quetzin started school to confirm his eligibility to take the bus, his bus number, and his drop off time. When I arrived at the transportation office I was very upset, as was Quetzin who arrived a few minutes later with tears running down his face. I proceeded to ask the transportation personnel why Quetzin was not dropped off at home. The lead bus driver for Quetzin's school said she had not provided Quetzin's home address to his bus driver because he was not eligible to take the bus. "Why is he not eligible to take the bus?" I asked. She replied, "Because he is a dual language student (a student participating in the dual language program as an English monolingual) and dual language students are not eligible for transportation." She went on to explain to me that his participation in the dual language program at his school is a choice and that he could attend his zoned school and be eligible for transportation. She confirmed his status in the program by asking me:

Lead Bus Driver:	He is not bilingual right?
Charise:	No. (He is Spanish monolingual).
Lead Bus Driver:	OK, yeah. Unless he is bilingual, he is not eligible to take the bus because attending the dual language program is a choice.
Charise:	Attending the dual language program is not a choice. His zoned school has no bilingual program whatsoever, and so all Spanish dominant students are automatically transferred out of that school and into a school that has a bilingual program [such as the dual language program at Quetzin's school].

In this narrative, we see how the transportation personnel utilized the discourse "White Americans are not bilingual" to make the decision that Quetzin was not eligible for transportation services. In the phone conversation I had had with the transportation personnel a week prior to Quetzin's first day of school, my ability to speak English fluently and without an accent must have signaled my racial identity as well as Quetzin's to the person I was talking to. Assuming that Quetzin and I were White, she reasoned that we were English-speaking monolinguals (informed by the discourse that White Americans are not bilingual). Thus, Quetzin's attendance of the dual language program, as a constructed White English-speaking monolingual student, was deemed optional, consequently disqualifying him from transportation services. When Quetzin and I arrived at the transportation office, I seemingly confirmed Quetzin's non-eligibility for transportation services. Upon seeing us, our racial identities confirmed that we were indeed White. Also, I spoke to the lead bus driver in English, so again she reasoned that Quetzin and I were English-speaking monolinguals. I seemed to confirm Quetzin's language status further when I told her he was not bilingual. I did not realize it at the time, but bilingual for them was coded as students who were Spanish speakers (bilingual or not). Not only was Quetzin assumed to be an English-speaking monolingual speaker, but that of the two sets of students attending the dual language program at his school (English monolingual and Spanish monolingual), only the Spanish monolingual students were being coded as bilingual. I was unable to convince the lead bus driver that Quetzin was indeed eligible for transportation services. The information she had gathered from us, including our White racial identity, my ability to speak English fluently, and my own admittance that Quetzin was not bilingual, permitted her to disqualify Quetzin from bus services, despite my objections. It was not until my husband and I went and talked to Quetzin's principal, explaining that Quetzin is participating in the dual language program as a Spanish-speaking monolingual, and her subsequent phone calls to the transportation office, that he was granted eligibility for bus services. The lead bus driver called me a week later to confirm Quetzin's eligibility to ride the bus due to his "bilingual" status. She stated, "I am so sorry about what happened on Monday. I have clarified with Quetzin's principal that he is a bilingual student and so he is eligible for bus service."

This practice of labeling only Spanish dominant students as bilinguals draws from and reproduces the discourses that White Americans are not bilingual and that languages are color-coded. The discourse that White Americans are not bilingual penetrates the logic of school practices, so much so that even when White students are in a bilingual program, they fail to be recognized as bilingual students. As we see from this narrative, the term bilingual is reserved for students who speak minority languages, who in actuality may not be any more bilingual than their English-speaking counterparts. This narrative clearly indicates that languages and bilingualism are color-coded.

IMPLICATIONS

These and other narratives emerge as my children and I speak (or do not speak) Spanish in public spaces. These narratives illustrate how bilingualism has been constructed in the United States to reflect a close association with race and language expectations we have of students. It is essential for teachers and other educators to be aware of these racially informed language expectations, both as a means to be critical of the deficit-oriented language programs and practices that are currently being implemented in many schools and to effectively build learning contexts that promote and sustain bilingualism for all students.

CONTRADICTIONS TO THESE LANGUAGE EXPECTATIONS

It is important for educators to know that at the same time school practices reproduce the racial discourses I have identified in this paper many students contradict these expectations. The discourses, languages are color-coded and White Americans are not bilingual, would have us believe that while White Americans speak English and English only, designated ethnic groups speak minority languages and are bilingual (e.g., Mexican Americans speak Spanish and English). In contrast to these discourses, as stated previously, many language minority students are participating in subtractive language programs (e.g., English Immersion, ESL, and TBE), thereby missing out on the opportunity to develop as bilingual learners. Moreover, increasing numbers of White, English-dominant parents are choosing to place their children in bilingual programs, as is indicated in the competitive nature of many dual language programs for English dominant students. Also, there are increasing numbers of ethnic/racial minority students (e.g., Latinos) who are entering schools as English monolinguals, some of whom occupy English dominant spaces in dual language programs. As a result of the complex language practices that both language minority and native English-speakers experience, in actuality it can be difficult to make any assumptions about language practices based on race.

HOW CAN WE PROMOTE BILINGUALISM FOR ALL STUDENTS DESPITE SOCIETY'S LANGUAGE EXPECTATIONS?

The racially informed expectations of who is or who should be bilingual may truncate teachers' as well as other educators' attempts to promote bilingualism for all students. The racially informed language expectations I have explained in this chapter assume that some ethnic minority populations (e.g., Latinos) are bilingual, when in reality societal pushes for English only and deficit-oriented language programs in schools make it difficult for Latino and other ethnic minority students to develop as bilingual learners. As educators, we need to be aware that society's expectations may not align with students' actual lived experiences, and so we need to find ways to ensure language minority students' bilingualism and not just assume that it will happen naturally, as suggested in the "languages are color-coded" discourse. Despite the language expectation that White students are not bilingual, White English-dominant students are participating in dual language programs in record numbers and achieve bilingualism and biliteracy after several years of being in the program. However, these gains in promoting bilingualism as a universal good for all students can be lost in a system that discursively produces White students as monolinguals even when they are in a bilingual program. As documented above, even those White English-dominant students who are participating in dual language programs can fail to be recognized as emerging bilinguals, as was the case in the dual language program my son is attending.

Given the history of bilingual education in this country, it is not surprising that language expectations and bilingualism have largely become tied to race. However, educators need to find ways to foster bilingualism for all students, despite these expectations. For language minority students and students who have lost the language of their abuelos/as, we need to enact school practices that encourage and validate students' existing and emerging bilingual development. When it comes to White students' developing bilingualism, educators should avoid the tendency to trivialize these students' bilingual efforts as honorary and exceptional rather than necessary and normal. This can be a difficult task in a society that does not currently understand the conception of White bilingualism.

CHAPTER THREE

Learning a Borderland Professional Identity

LINDA GUARDIA JACKSON, SHEILA BERNAL GUZMAN, &
GUADALUPE RAMOS

A mother says to her son as she leaves him at the door, "*Adios mi amor, te portas bien*" (Good-bye my love, behave well). This loving farewell message from a mother to her son raises many questions. What does it mean to "behave well" in the context of the public school classroom? What does it mean to the institution and what does it mean to the family? What is considered "behaving well" regardless of the explicit rules that are ubiquitously posted in every classroom? Does it mean that you compete to be the best in the class? Does it mean you help fellow students with their work? There is a significant difference between the English word *education* and the Spanish *educación*. Education tends to refer to formal schooling. It is a component of *educación*. Although formal schooling is a part of *educación*, the concept of educación is more complex. It involves responsibility and respect, as well as a collectivist orientation toward family and community. This mother's loving farewell calls for reflection on the funds of knowledge or cultural resources that the child brings, but also very importantly what the teacher brings.

As three *comadres* involved for many years in bilingual education, we believe that an understanding of self is crucial to the work that teachers do. This understanding includes a "conception of self as socially, racially, and culturally constructed." We engage with this "pedagogy of identity" through telling stories of our involvement in bilingual education. First, we provide a historical context for our experiences. Next, we place ourselves in this context through our *historias y cuentos*. We continue by discussing the initiation and process of our dialoguing. Finally, we conclude with implications for bilingual educators (Jenlink, 2006, p. 126).

BACKGROUND

The intersection of race/ethnicity, gender, class, immigration, generational position, and language forms the basis of the complex experiences of Mexican Americans growing up and living in Texas. Many in this group, including Mexican American bilingual educators (MABEs), have advocated for justice and equality through the reformation of education. This fight has continued for decades. Nevertheless, there still exists an academic imbalance that puts Latina/o students at a disadvantage (Darder, 1991; Romo & Falbo, 1996; Valencia, 2002 & 2005; Valenzuela, 1999).

A major challenge in educating this student population concerns bilingual education. The students' experiences are well documented in numerous studies aimed at deciphering and explaining how best to educate this group. Much less attention has been paid to Mexican American teachers' daily experiences impacting her/his trajectory of identity formation in the social and cultural contexts of bilingual education. Since, ultimately, the teacher delivers the curriculum that is essential to their students' learning, the educational process is in large part determined by the teacher's sense of identity. As Galindo relate, "The manner in which minority teachers sort out and interpret their cultural identity plays a crucial role in their identity as educators" (p. 51). Thus, we turn to the identity and agency of MABEs to examine intra- and inter-personal dynamics, which can influence pedagogical practices when working with students of Mexican descent (Holland et al., 1998; Galindo & Olguin, 1996; Quiocho & Rios, 2000).

We have come to realize that identity consciousness is inextricably intertwined with teacher transformation and both serve as essential ingredients in any educational innovation such as bilingual education. This leads to our view that teacher transformation is a process that involves reflection and dialogue wherein the examination of cumulative life experiences can provide *apoyo* or support and impact instructional philosophies and practices for teachers serving culturally and linguistically diverse students and parents (Saavedra, 1995; Galindo & Olguin, 1996).

We contend that a teacher's *conocimiento* of self is as essential as the implementation of the model itself. Toward this end, we move away from more traditional studies of the challenges of the education of culturally and linguistically diverse (CLD) students to an examination of the interaction and transformation of ethnic and professional identities of teachers serving those students in the context of public education. Our goal is to provide MABEs with a framework to navigate and negotiate between their ethnic and professional identities to provide additive, enriched instruction for the population they serve.

HISTORIAS Y CUENTOS

As a way to support each other and tease out an understanding of the complexities entailed in being a MABE, the three of us have been telling and listening to each other's stories for 25 years. Connelly and Clandinin (2000) explain, "We live in a world of stories, and though we help shape those stories, we are shaped by them" (p. 318). Through our storytelling, although we did not realize it initially, we were seeking self-understanding of our lived experiences. These ongoing conversations have provided a space to dialogue about selfhood, assumptions, and beliefs. The dialogic process of sharing our *historias y cuentos* has afforded us the counterstories[1] so important to the affirmation and validation of our pedagogy and practice.

Linda

> *In my early years, I was not allowed to speak Spanish at school and not encouraged to speak it at home. I consciously made an effort later in life to learn the language that my grandparents and my parents spoke. Since I had been unable to have a lengthy conversation with my monolingual Spanish-speaking grandmother while I was growing up, I never got to hear her cuentos directly from her. I know that she had many stories to tell because my mother has told them to me over the years. This saddens me to this day.*

Lupe

> *So I was born in Eagle Pass. I have interesting memories of my childhood. Mainly, there were some good times. But think what helps me be a good bilingual teacher is that I had interesting situations that happened to me when I was little. I remember very clearly those times. I think the reason I remember clearly is because some of them were traumatic. Especially, I remember going into an all-English classroom.*

Sheila

> *The Spanish language and culture are important parts of my childhood memories. My older sister and I spoke Spanish growing up. When my older sister Elizabeth started school my parents and paternal grandparents (in broken English, as Spanish was their primary language), and my uncles who spoke English well, began speaking English to us. In time we "lost" our Spanish speaking skills so that when my maternal grandmother came to visit or to stay with us, my sisters and I were unable to communicate with her. She spoke only Spanish. She would complain to my mother and to us about our inability to speak Spanish. I know about language loss, as do my sisters.*

We shared daily events and interactions, such as familial warmth and closeness, conflict, slights, and discriminations that have formed us. Sharing our stories has been central in the formation of our identities. We realize now that our *cuentos* have helped to shape our ways of being and ways of knowing.

FORMALIZING THE PROCESS

Luis Urrieta argues that our historical moment calls for critical awareness wherein "day to day practice is embedded with the hope for a domino effect or a ripple effect to bring about larger societal change" (p. 183). We agree with Freire when he states, "...activity consists of action and reflection: it is praxis; it is transformation of the world" (p. 119). He connects action and reflection with dialogue when he explains, "Dialogue is the encounter in which the united reflection and action of the dialoguers are addressed to the world which is to be transformed and humanized" (p. 88). With this in mind, we formalized a method to dialogue about our early experiences, schooling, and teaching (Freire, 2000; Urrieta, 2005).

We conducted three-way dialogues about our life histories, our experiences as MABEs implementing a dual language Montessori model, as well as the local, state, and national contexts of bilingual education. We structured this dialogic method by journaling through email. We call it our "Dialogue Ejournal."[2] This process, focused on autobiographical accounts, began in September 2007. However, our conversations go back several years. Therefore, we include excerpts from our ejournal triad, as well as previous conversations to answer the question: *How does dialoguing about ethnic identity, professional identity, knowledge, and experience shape what it means to be a Latina educator in Texas?* The question emerges from our experiences as MABEs involved in the implementation of Montessori-based dual language programs. Through our discussions three themes arose: transformational self-determination, *conocimiento con cariño,* and border crossing.

TRANSFORMATIONAL SELF-DETERMINATION

Dialoguing about our different lived experiences led each of us very early in our careers to transformational self-determination, whereby we rejected the subtractive schooling that we were subjected to and embraced additive bilingual education. Additive bilingual education goes by many names such as dual language, two-way, one-way, language immersion, maintenance bilingual, developmental bilingual, and late-exit. Whatever the label, the goal is the same—an enriched education to achieve academically in two languages. The vision is to value both the home language and English in culturally respectful ways to foster academic excellence (Torres-Guzman, 2002; Valenzuela, 1999).

CONOCIMIENTO CON CARIÑO

First, through the network that we established among ourselves, we recognized that our shared *cuentos* helped us commit to the concept of additive bilingual education and the importance of maintaining Spanish. Then, our search began for a pedagogy that was more culturally appropriate for students of Mexican origin. As Arce (2004) maintains, "A major challenge for bilingual educators is to critically reevaluate the limitations of maintaining traditional pedagogies that appear to benefit only some children" (p. 232). We wanted to be inclusive of the students and our own cultural values and resources. This led to our attraction to Montessori evolving from what we call *conocimiento con cariño*. This construct is embedded in Angela Valenzuela's argument that the socialization of Mexican children leads to the embracing of learning and academic achievement within the context of nurturing and mentoring relations. Thus, we came to the Montessori method because of our ways of knowing with caring, but at different times. Linda speaks to this in one of her responses:

> My first reading of Freire's *Pedagogy of the Oppressed* led me to search for methods of education alternative to the "banking" concept. My goal was to find an alternative means to teaching CLD students because it was obvious to me that the way it was being done was not working for a large number of children. I ultimately chose the Montessori method as being a viable option that combined theory with practice which closely matched Freire's idea of a "problem posing" approach to education (Guardia Jackson, September 15, 2007).

A basic premise, foundational to our "ways of knowing," is a profound belief in the goodness and potential of each child. As Sheila states:

> I believe in the inherent goodness of the individual. I also believe in equity and social justice. I have experienced being marginalized and have witnessed others who have also been marginalized. I have been powerless and have witnessed others who have been powerless. I have been silenced and witnessed others who have been silenced. And so out of those varied experiences has grown a desire for me to value and promote equity, inclusiveness, collaboration, and discourse (Guzman, October 5, 2007).

We continue to promote and implement dual language programs, jointly and individually, despite numerous obstacles and barriers in our determination to provide an enriched, additive education for CLD students.

BORDER CROSSINGS

An examination of our *cuentos* created an awareness of an emergent theme of how our identities were impacted by crossing multiple borders. Our attempts at combining dual language and Montessori in the public schools created instances of constant border crossings of competing discourses. Lupe points out:

> When I'm at the public schools, I'm seen as a Montessori teacher that does things in the classroom. When I'm with Montessori teachers, I'm seen as a public school teacher who doesn't do the method completely (Ramos, September 12, 2007).

However, our border crossings entail more than educational methods and pedagogies. Besides living at the geographical U.S./Mexican border, we live at cultural borderlands and experience "the effects of multiple colonizations—including the Spanish legacy, United States imperialism, Mexican nationalisms and global patriarchy and heterosexism." Through our border crossings, we strive to create "a new *mestiza consciousness, una conciencia de mujer.* It is a consciousness of the Borderlands" (Anzaldúa, 1999, p. 99; Elenes et al., 2001, p. 598).

Our shared experiences of networking, dialoguing, and authoring of our lived personal and professional experiences through *cuentos* have provided the sustenance in our trajectory toward forging our personal and professional identities as MABEs. Furthermore, as we have illustrated with excerpts from our ejournaling process, these are effective strategies that we recommend to MABEs—pre-service, novice, or veteran—that produce powerful, transformative insights.

IMPLICATIONS

Studies show that for minority group teachers personal and professional identities are linked. The shaping of a professional identity is connected to schooling experiences as well as teaching experiences. This happens in the social, historical, and cultural context of family, school, and community. Further, the professional identity of some MABEs is constructed and reconstructed through the practice of bilingual education within the context of a lack of bilingual education in early life. Therefore, we advocate that bilingual education teachers know their stories well, share stories, and listen to others' stories. Grounded in our own experiences, our *consejos* are focused on networking, dialogue, and *cuentos.* These processes can be utilized to lead to praxis through reflection and action (Allexsaht-Snider, 1996; Galindo & Olguin, 1996; Quiocho & Rios, 2000).

NETWORKING

The value of networking has received considerable attention and study. Networking for teachers has recently been formalized to include mentoring programs, peer mentoring, master teacher support, instructional coaching, instructional specialist assistance, and a number of other strategies. Because of the unique positions of MABEs who seek to craft their professional and personal identities within the hegemony of existing educational policy practice, networking takes a unique form (Nieto, 2003; Zalaquett & Lopez, 2006). The type of networking that we have experienced and that we recommend is characterized as follows:

1. Networks are formed with individuals inside and outside formal organizational structures;
2. Networks maintain an intimate and reflective group of 3–5 to facilitate the creating, sharing, and reflecting of *cuentos y testimonios;*
3. Networks of MABEs strive to create and maintain larger networks outside the small, intimate group;
4. MABE networks establish a flexible process for dialoguing through *cuentos;* and
5. MABE networks design plans of action in areas of collaborative need or concern.

In summary, the MABE network is dynamic, personal, flexible, and above all collaborative. Once established, the network is uniquely characterized by the essence of the *comadrazo* or *compadrazo* concept. It is stable and yet fluid, it is supportive and yet challenging, it is collaborative and yet personal. The type of network we subscribe to supports the construction of both personal and professional identities.

DIALOGUING

The dialogic process we recommend for MABEs is characterized by a process for the input of ideas, active listening by all participants, reflection on commentary presented, and purposeful response to the input of others. When we began our dialoguing, we came up with a list of questions and topics. Our questions served only as prompts. This process, by whatever method, can serve several purposes in guiding classroom practice: by assisting in the continuous development of a philosophy of bilingual education; by assisting bilingual teachers in understanding the concept of bilingualism and multiculturalism; by lessening the sense of isolation that some novice bilingual teachers experience; by assisting in retention of bilingual teachers in the classroom; and by preparing pre-service teachers to serve CLD students.

STORYTELLING

The crafting and sharing of our *cuentos* has proven to be cathartic in the process of our shared MABE experience. We consider this strategy as essential because of the liberating impact that each experienced. The use of the *cuento* strategy by MABEs illuminates the similarities and differences that are important in our transformative self-determination. The power of narrative storytelling is strong because it provides a previously denied space for expressing who we are and what we have experienced. The storytelling occurs in our network's shared space where we can receive and perceive *cuentos* from an assets-based perspective, rather than a deficit-based perspective.

PRAXIS

For bilingual educators, we contend that the use of the strategies of networking, dialoguing, and *cuentos* will result in assisting with the process of moving along a trajectory of private and professional identity creation. Specifically, bilingual educators will be aided in their efforts to establish a coherent and effective philosophy of bilingual education. This clearer vision of what is relevant bilingual education and what it means to be an effective bilingual educator will impact instruction and Latino student achievement. With a clearer perspective, MABEs will be equipped with the confidence and vision to critically reflect, collaborate, strategize, and implement corrective actions needed to effectively meet the educational needs of the students that they serve. With knowledge of professional and personal selves, acquired through the suggested strategies, MABEs will be moved to action with the critical consciousness to challenge and rectify the most daunting issues facing Latina/o students (Freire, 2000).

CONCLUSION

When writing about their work with teacher knowledge, Connelly and Clandinin (1999) noticed that teachers' questions were about identity. "They were questions of 'Who am I in my story of teaching?' 'Who am I in my administrator's stories?' 'Who am I in parents' stories?' and so on" (p. 3). We realize that we are works in progress with multiple identities. Further, we continue to come to understandings about what is "self," "selfhood," and "identity," and how it is produced. We agree with Holland and others (1998) when they state:

> People tell others who they are, but even more important, they tell themselves and then try to act as though they are who they say they are. These self understandings, especially those with strong emotional resonance for the teller, are what we refer to as identities (p.3).

Telling *nuestros cuentros*, as well as critical analysis of assumptions and beliefs about bilingualism and biliteracy can contribute to constructing and reconstructing identity and agency of bilingual educators.

As long as a person is alive, identity production is in process and unfinished. The formation of MABEs' identities encompasses issues such as colonization, marginalization, assimilation, and accommodation. By focusing on the cultural means and historical conditions, as well as the events and environments of a bilingual teacher in bilingual education, the constant refiguring of self brings attention to the concept of multiple selves in process. This perspective considers that we are not reproducing ourselves and our culture; rather, we appropriate, produce, and improvise, allowing for the possibility of transformation.

NOTES

1. A counterstory is an alternative narrative to recount experiences of marginalization and resistance (Yosso, 2006).
2. This idea is based on the work of Dr. Sofia Villenas and Linda Prieto with paired (auto)biographical dialogues.

CHAPTER FOUR

Nuyorican

ALMA RUBAL-LOPEZ

Language is one of the major factors that differentiate humans from other living species of animals. One cannot conceive of civilization without its presence; in fact thought without language is most likely improbable. Furthermore, language makes possible the transmission of our deepest, most intimate and most complex thoughts and feelings. A common language has the capacity to bring people from different cultures, socioeconomic strata and races together in a manner unlike any other means. It also provides us with the capacity to describe the theoretical in concrete ways, allowing us to make sense of the universe. Language is at the essence of our existence, and life without it is inconceiveable. Nevertheless, language also has the power to divide people, isolate them, be at the root of turmoil, and human suffering.

Not surprisingly, language played a significant role in forming my identity and that of my sister. Angie and I were born in New York City during the 1950s and 1960s. Our generation paved the way for subsequent immigrant populations from the Caribbean, Latin America, and other non-European countries that settled in New York City. The term Nuyorican is used to describe this generation of Puerto Ricans born in New York. Our presence was critical in helping to define issues of race, assimilation, and equity never before confronted by immigrants (African Americans notwithstanding) who were not white Europeans in a society that defined itself as a "melting pot." As cited in Anselmo & Rubal-Lopez (2005):

We were the ones who fought against being placed into traditional categories of race. We were the ones who paved the way for subsequent immigrants of color. We were the ones who refused to lose our language despite the consequences. We were the ones who embraced being referred to as "persons of color." We were also the ones who were met with skepticism and criticism by those whom we expected to be accepting of us.

One of the ways that my generation differentiated itself was through language. Language was a marker of who we were. This helped define us in a world that was a racial dichotomy of "black" or "white." We were different and our language allowed us to convey this. We might look "black" or "white," but the minute we spoke in Spanish, you knew that we were Puerto Rican. In essence, language was our marker and still continues to be.

It has provided me with the key to succeeding in the classroom, working in a professional domain and has allowed me to function in other domains that necessitate the use of clear and accurate language such as in court, banking or medicine. However, language has also served as a marker to be used against me, as a rationale for tracking me in school, as a means to associate me with being Puerto Rican and all the negative stereotypes that accompany that association, and as a reason for excluding me from different circles. In essence, the power of language is great but language is a double-edged sword. It can be one's greatest support and a major vehicle in helping one succeed. However, it can also be the source of great grief in one's life.

I truly feel that there are great advantages in being bilingual, and I truly believe that knowing more than one language enriches your life. Not only can you understand, enjoy and appreciate the music, literature, and culture of many countries as in the case of Spanish, but there are also cognitive advantages that have been found in bilinguals. Cognitive flexibility, earlier meta-linguistic awareness in young children, and higher scores in some subtests found in IQ tests are some of the many advantages. Moreover, there are many career opportunities for persons who can speak more than one language. Our technological world has brought countries closer together in ways that were unimaginable 50 years ago. Our global economy and our constant intercommunications make bilingualism a commodity and one that can enhance our career opportunities.

Most importantly, language is about who you are. It is part of one's identity and defines us. Language allows one to maintain ethnic ties with family members. It is very sad to witness immigrant parents who have lost communication with their children because their young have lost their ethnic tongue, and their parents have not acquired English. As a young social worker in the South Bronx, I would oftentimes witness the disintegration of an entire family as the lines of communication would become weaker and weaker as English entered the lives of the young and the elderly were left speaking in Spanish. The linguistic distance would ultimately translate into emotional and psychological distance and the subsequent isolation of family members.

On a personal level, it was very difficult for me to communicate with my father since he did not speak in English; also to maintain family ties as well as communication with predominately Spanish-speaking persons who care for my father in Puerto Rico. While the advantages of knowing two languages are many, becoming bilingual and maintaining the use of these two languages is not easily attained in a country that does not value or promulgate bilingualism.

My parents were faced with difficult decisions of what language(s) to use at home. As a young child, I can recall my parents' discussions on the matter of speaking between my Spanish-speaking father and my English/Spanish-speaking bilingual mother. Their linguistic dilemma reflects the views and conflicts that many Puerto Ricans confronted when they immigrated to the United States. As the first large wave of Spanish-speaking immigrant persons of color at a time in the United States when the melting pot philosophy was prevalent, we were faced with issues of race, ethnicity, class and language. My parents' views about language are best described in the following excerpt taken from mine and my sister's book, *On Becoming Nuyoricans* (p. 115, 2005):

> The power of language and its role in determining one's status in American society were well understood by both our parents. Nonetheless, each had his/her own perspective about English and the role that it should play in the lives of their two girls.
>
> My father, who was involved with the nationalist movement of Puerto Rico and was as anti-American as you could be without being a terrorist, refused to speak English in the home. He feared having children who did not speak Spanish. His stance on speaking Spanish at home was based on ideological reasons, while my mother's choice to speak English at home was based on social mobility and her need to protect us. My mother was very aware of the codes of power that are played out in school and the disadvantages that a child has if he does not possess this code (Delpit, 1995).
>
> She witnessed the very difficult time that Angela had because she only spoke in Spanish when she first entered school, so she decided to speak to us in English. My mother's education, which consisted of a high school education in Puerto Rico during a time that the Island's language policy dictated the use of English in school, provided her with that option. Needless to say that this choice was not available to many of my friends' parents who only spoke Spanish.
>
> Our home's linguistic repertoire consisted of both my parents speaking in two different languages when addressing us, the use of Spanish when speaking to one another and our code switching when speaking to both of them.
>
> Both approaches have had their impact on our lives. The use of English at home did provide us with the linguistic code necessary for academic achievement. This was an advantage that many of our Spanish dominant friends with monolingual parents with less education did not have. Our English competency has allowed us to compete and succeed in the academic and professional environment oftentimes restricted to those who have not been privy to this code. We have not suffered the shame and negative consequences of being labeled

"limited English proficient," "uneducable," "stupid," or any of the many harmful and derogatory categories reserved for those who do not speak English. In fact, our success as students and also as professionals in the workplace has very often been interpreted as stemming from various sources while overlooking what may be the most important, namely, our knowledge of the dominant language. We have at times been revered as persons who are the exception when possibly language might be the underlying factor in our success.

On the other hand, the Spanish spoken by us has never reached native-like competency. While we can carry on a conversation and function in any Spanish-speaking environment, English is the language that we feel most comfortable with when writing and performing any kind of academic work or official function. Our apparent dominance in English has led to our being criticized by those who perceive this as "trying to be Americana," while there are still those who must let us know when speaking Spanish that our pronunciation or incorrect usage is not of a native speaker.

Our mixture of Spanish and English, also referred to as Spanglish, is seen as an inferior code. The lack of native-like Spanish competency has been a marker for our not being "true Puerto Ricans" and our subsequent exclusion from certain circles reserved for such individuals. The irony of this is that those engaged in the labeling have often been Puerto Ricans who are in pursuit of maintaining their language and culture, but who have often dealt with the "Nuyorican" in a prejudicial, exclusionary and elitist manner and have unwittingly become the oppressor. Our experiences were those of marginalized persons who were living in two worlds (Stonequist, 1961; Zentella, 1997; Villanueva, 1993).

When I was young, I remember my father warning my mother about speaking to us in English and the loss of Spanish that would ultimately occur if she continued to do so. I remember resenting my father's stance about speaking in Spanish, and recall my own negative sentiments regarding my father's limited use and knowledge of English. I was embarrassed that he spoke broken incomprehensible English. My father's limited English was a marker of what he was—Puerto Rican, not "truly American"—and the negative stereotypes in a society that frowned on being Puerto Rican. I remember wanting to avoid being in my father's position, and every time my father spoke in English, he was pulling me in the opposite direction that I wished to go. There were times that I hated myself for feeling this way about my father and ultimately about who I was, but that feeling was too often present, in particular, in the presence of non-Latino persons who I felt were the ones who were making those judgments.

I also knew how awful it was in school for children who could not speak English. They always seemed lost and never understood what was going on and I did not want that for myself. They were the misfits academically and disadvantaged and often socially isolated. Much of how these students were perceived was driven by our teachers' perceptions. Educators saw themselves as having the mission of making these children English speakers, and one logical way was to ignore their native language and culture. This lack of validation for who these students were or from where they came was interpreted by all of us as a defect with who they were and what they represented, namely, un-American. This thrust to become an American was powerful. We, as children, not only strove to attain the American dream but also accepted the idea that in order to do so, one's ethnicity should also disappear. If my parents had not maintained their language and culture, I would not be writing about the importance of language in my life. To be in pursuit of the American dream and to faithfully adhere to what I was told I needed to do to succeed, I would today be monolingual English speaking with a very different identity.

Linguistic concerns became central in the formation of my identity during the summer between sixth and seventh grades. My parents separated and my mother took my sister, Angie, and me to Puerto Rico. What I never expected was that one day my poor Spanish language skills would put me in a situation comparable to those of students who could not speak English in the United States. Language became a very huge issue when selecting a school because we did not know how to read and write in Spanish. My mother placed us in a Catholic school where some of the curriculum was taught in English and some in Spanish. Public school was out of the question because Spanish was the medium of instruction for all subjects. Here, I experienced firsthand the desperate feeling of not being able to express myself, of being different, and being singled out as a "gringa." I now knew what it meant to be isolated and marginalized. I found myself in Puerto Rico, not being accepted as a Puerto Rican, and coming from New York where I was not seen as being American. Hence, the Nuyorican identity emerged.

Prior to living in Puerto Rico, I could not conceive why I should know Spanish and the impact that knowing a second language would have on my life and identity. It never occurred to me that my relationship with my parents, in particular my father, who did not speak English very well, would be very different if I did not speak Spanish. The transmittal of my parents' knowledge, values and wisdom would have never occurred had I not understood Spanish. Without my father's expansive knowledge of world history and his personal analysis of events, I would have been deficient in knowing much of the history that is excluded in our Eurocentric curriculum. The intimacy stemming from shared feelings and emotions would also be missing from my life, hence, wedging a distance between my parents and myself.

Without knowing Spanish I would also be incapable of transmitting a second language to my children and providing them with a cultural legacy that they, too, could appreciate and by which their lives would be enriched. I am very grateful for my father's insistence on speaking to me in Spanish for I would not be who I am today without this very important part of who I am.

For current immigrants in the United States, language issues also play a crucial role in their lives. Current immigrants find themselves torn between nationalism and globalization. They wish to become Americans but also recognize the advantages of being able to function in various languages in a world driven by electronic communication and instant messaging. Very often the continual use of the native language is interpreted as being resistant to becoming American while the immigrant sees it as a necessity to function in two worlds.

Although the melting pot view of American society has been replaced with a view of a "salad bowl" or "mosaic," the linguistic component of American society remains very similar to that encountered by the Nuyorican, namely, English is used in official domains while ethnic languages are used at home and continue not to be supported in school. One difference is that with the increase of television, radio, email and other technological means of communication, English now extensively permeates the home more easily. Nonetheless, the stigma of knowing another language is not as great as it was when I was a child.

The linguistic patterns of newcomers in the United States remain the same as that for past immigrants. By the third generation, complete linguistic acculturation has occurred. That is, the immigrant language is replaced by the exclusive use of English. Traditionally, the first generation is characterized by the use of the ethnic mother tongue at home, followed by the use of both English and the immigrant tongue by the second generation, then by the exclusive use of English by members of the third generation. In some cases, this shift occurs within one generation. In essence, many children of immigrants find themselves English monolinguals without any knowledge of their parents' mother tongue, and the following generations are most probably speakers of only one language, namely, English (Rubal-Lopez, 1994).

Unlike past immigrants who left their homeland with an understanding that they most likely would never return, our current population not only maintain communication with those left behind in the homeland but very often return to visit their country of origin. In order to maintain these ties, decisions regarding what language(s) should be transmitted to their offspring are as important as any other issue regarding their children's development.

For those who are parents, concerns of English acquisition and transmittal of the native language to their offspring are major considerations. Although they wish to acquire English as quickly as possible, they also realize the necessity of maintaining their ethnic ties in a world driven by a global economy and immediate transnational communication via email, jet, and telephone.

When making language choices, many immigrant parents would like to see their children fluent in both English and their mother tongue. The fact that we perceive the United States as a multilingual democratic society often leads these parents to conclude that it is not only possible to raise their children speaking two languages but that this process is one that is compatible and easily attainable in our multicultural and free society. In essence, many believe that if they wish to have bilingual offspring, all that needs to be done is to speak to their children in two languages, assuming that they speak two languages. If the parents are not English speakers then school will take care of the teaching of English to their children, and the immigrant language can be transmitted at home.

However, development of bilingualism in the United States is not an easy feat. The forces impacting what language a child will acquire and retain are many and often fall outside the realm of the parents' purview. Issues of status, function, and societal allocations of a language lie at the heart of why it is so difficult to retain two languages in the United States. English, with a high status and functions associated with prestige, wealth and power, is the language associated with progress and social mobility, while the use of the immigrant language is relegated to functions of the home and sometimes church. English also enjoys a global dispersion unlike that of any other language in the history of mankind, putting into question the need for two languages. Furthermore, philosophical concerns regarding national unity and loyalty add to the mix of the multitude of forces that impact on language choice in our country.

Despite the upward climb to maintain and transmit their mother tongue faced by current immigrants in the United States, I would encourage all to do so. However, this will only be possible with a clear and steadfast parental vision. Compartmentalization of languages in the home and continual opportunities in different domains for the use of the ethnic tongue will be crucial in attaining this feat. The struggle is difficult but the payoff is priceless.

Language should not be seen as a dividing force, rather as a means to comprehend and bring persons together. Being educated should never be frowned upon; knowing two languages is exactly that. Doing so provides us with the ability to understand other cultures, have greater insight into human behavior and, most importantly, the capacity to understand from where we came in order to appreciate who we are.

CHAPTER FIVE

Whitestreaming

Why Some Latinas/os Fear Bilingual Education

LUIS URRIETA, JR.

Mexican Americans are not the only groups who have lobbied for and have used bilingual education programs U.S. in history, in the current context, bilingual education is most closely associated with this group (Gutierrez & Jaramillo, 2006).

While some Mexican Americans argue against bilingual education as a barrier to economic opportunities, in this chapter I argue that Mexican Americans that fear bilingual education, from a cultural perspective, suffer from the effects of whitestreaming. Whitestreaming is akin to uncritical assimilation, or cultural genocide. Whitestreaming is a coercive force that imposes White history, mores, morals, language, customs, individualism, cultural capital and other forces as the norm or standard U.S. in society. It is argued by whitestreamers, in teleological fashion, that the whitestream represents the epitome of civilization, development, and democracy, as well as the superiority of English over Spanish. In schools, whitestreaming translates into whitestream curricula (what is taught) and whitestream pedagogy (how children are taught—or not) (Urrieta, 2004a).

Without a doubt, issues of bilingual education, Latina/o identity, and the education of Latina/o children in the whitestream system are difficult to sort. When I first began working as a bilingual teacher, I was unsure I agreed with what I was doing in my bilingual classroom. In many ways, I disagreed with bilingual education, and yet I was paid to do something with which I did not completely agree. Interestingly, I did not even know what bilingual education was really about. I will share pieces of my own story throughout this chapter, not for self-indulgence, but because it is the story with which I am most familiar.

GUILTY

Generally, in whitestream American culture we are taught to associate bilingual education with remedial education. I am guilty because I, too, believed this whitestream notion. I had not been taught bilingually as a child—so my assumptions were mostly shaped by the whitestream discourse—that bilingual education was not looked upon favorably. I struggled with my action as a teacher, but in hindsight, I struggled mostly because I did not know what I was doing—period. Until two months before I became a bilingual teacher, I still was unsure of my career aspirations. In fact, when I decided to become a bilingual teacher, I was hired on a Thursday and started teaching classes the following Monday—on an emergency permit (González Baker, 1996).

All I needed to be a bilingual teacher in California, in 1995, was to have a B.A. degree and pass a test with a multiple choice section and two short essays. Although, for the most part, while bilingual educators may have begun with good intentions, I am amazed that the students who needed the most well-trained and experienced teachers got people like me who had no idea what we were doing in a classroom. I really had no idea what I was doing—I lacked classroom management skills and seriously considered quitting in the beginning.

Later, I began to question whether it was my lack of skills that made teaching difficult, or whether it was also my negative attitude toward my students. I tended to see my students through a deficit lens. In my mind, the list of my students' deficiencies was long. I kept trying to compare myself with them when I was their age—which was an unfair and ageist comparison. I also never stopped to ask myself what they brought to the classroom. What did my students know? What skills did they have that I was overlooking?

The worst thing is I, too, bought into having low expectations of them. I bought into the discourse that they were lazy, though some were; but most were not. I also bought into the discourse that maybe their parents did not care about their education. Slowly, however, I came to realize most of my students were among the most intelligent, respectful, dignified, diligent people I had ever met. I also realized that most of their parents were some of the most hardworking, concerned, and friendly people I ever encountered. Sadly, when we have stereotypes about people, we tend to always look for the examples that confirm the stereotypes—rather than the many examples that disprove it.

REALIZATION

In order to keep our jobs as bilingual teachers, our emergency teaching permits required that we take classes toward full teacher certification. I began taking education classes at night at Cal State L.A. that included bilingual theory classes, English as a Second Language, classroom management, and others. Some classes were more valuable to me than others, while some merely required a lot of busy work such as lesson plans, teaching statements, and other assignments that seemed irrelevant to me because I was already teaching. In time, I began to be a more efficient teacher, though not necessarily a better teacher.

In the summer of 1997, however, I attended a three-week seminar on teaching using critical pedagogy. This experience drastically changed my perspective on teaching—especially having learned the banking approach (a deficiency perspective on students). I challenged myself by taking the Spanish version of the seminar which really changed my outlook on bilingual education. I left the seminar a believer in bilingual education and critical pedagogy. For the first time I could not wait for the school year to start. I became enthusiastic about teaching. I began to care about my students with genuine cariño, and not just in superficial ways (Valenzuela, 1999).

At the seminar we read *Pedagogía del Oprimido* (*Pedagogy of the Oppressed* by Paulo Freire, 1970) and my outlook on teaching continued to change. I learned how to engage in dialogue and to value my students' experiences. I learned to draw on my students' prior knowledge and to use poetry, el arte de la declamación, writer's workshop, and la silla del autor. Most importantly, I learned to value my students' multiple uses of language.

After the seminar on Freire, many components of my classroom changed and I observed a new sense of student learning beginning. Not that I did not have success with a few students during my first years of teaching, but I can honestly say, with an element of shame, that those first groups of students I taught were successful despite my ways of teaching and despite my views of them and their realities. I also became more of a facilitator. I was not afraid to let students decide what interested them, and the students began to read, question, and be more assertive. They were already proud of who they were (in ways that I was not while I was growing up) and they became more critical of the system and resourceful in how to negotiate that system.

After the seminar, I also started to reflect on my own experiences—both as a student and as a teacher. I asked myself, what was different about my students' experiences and my own experience? It was then that I realized that growing up I had been infected with a terrible disease many Mexican Americans and other Latinas/os suffer(ed) from. It is an emotionally and psychologically debilitating disease that a lot of people have and don't even realize it. This disease is a by-product of racism and ethnocentrism. This disease has been called internalized oppression and is the result of whitestreaming in society—especially in schools.

Internalized oppression is when we, as so-called minorities, learn to accept negative views of ourselves and our own people. Subsequently we internalize whitestream views and learn to dislike our own selves, our own cultures, our own identities, and our own languages. Internalized oppression sometimes turns into hate of those that represent what we dislike the most about ourselves. People of color heavily burdened with internalized oppression also sometimes become the strongest proponents for whitestreaming, though ironically it is sometimes critically conscious White people who struggle to fight against whitestream indoctrination.

Growing up, I once had deficit views about my own people, my culture, my first language, and my second language. I felt that my English was not as proficient as it could have been because I spoke Spanish first. I learned to see myself as deficient and disadvantaged. I had started to deal with these issues in college—but not realizing just how bad my case of internalized oppression was until I was teaching in a bilingual classroom.

Learning to Unlearn the Whitestream

I had to unlearn many of my whitestream misconceptions—which I would challenge anyone, but especially Latinas/os opposing bilingual education, to do. The first whitestream misconception I unlearned was about language. I had to unlearn that the Spanish language is somehow an obstacle or disadvantage. People who view Spanish as a deficit probably do not know the language well enough to make that judgment. Spanish is a beautiful language with a rich history of literacy, literature, and culture. Deficit views of Spanish are still a common whitestream misconception. I recently read applications for scholarships targeting "Hispanic" students within which applicants were asked to write an essay describing an obstacle that they had to overcome. An overwhelming number of students wrote that speaking Spanish was an obstacle. Still, instead of seeing the Spanish language as a resource, we are taught to see this as an impediment. For example, there are so many cognates that translate in science since so much of the language of science is based on Latin. Spanish can be quite useful in developing biliteracies in students and yet students are taught by whitestream standards to forget Spanish, the sooner the better. Joel Dworin (2003) aptly argues that developing biliteracy requires bidirectionality that needs to be viewed from a bilingual rather than a whitestream (monolingual) lens. Simultaneous multilingual language development is not a detriment or disadvantage, rather an advantage. But we are coerced by the whitestream not to see it that way (Bravo, Hiebert, & Pearson, 2007).

In Europe and other parts of the world, children grow up speaking three, four, or five different languages. It is a matter of cultural genocide that the whitestream uses linguicism (or linguistic racism) as a way to coerce Mexican American children and other second language students to speak English only. There is not anything innately deficient about second language students, and no one is arguing that these students should not learn English. However, we continue to be coerced into thinking that there is enough room in their brains for only one language (Skutnabb-Kangas, 2000).

Speaking Spanish, or any other language, does not inhibit your ability to learn English or several other languages. If anything, solid bilingual instruction with well-trained, fully-certified, competent bilingual teachers makes learning multiple languages one of this nation's strongest assets. But instead we are led to believe in whitestream views that Spanish, and other languages, are hindrances.

The second whitestream misconception I unlearned in my self-reflection process while teaching was that I had to constantly struggle against the damage of internalized oppression in terms of my cultural identity. I realized that growing up, often in order to feel better about myself as a Mexican American, I was implicitly and sometimes explicitly taught that being Mexican (from Mexico) was an unfavorable identity. In order to feel better about ourselves (as U.S.-born Mexican Americans), we were taught to rid ourselves of all things that were "too Mexican," and make fun of ourselves. We learned to say things like "so Mexican!" or in California we used to say "so TJ!" "TJ" stood for Tijuana, the closest border town that represented what we did not want to be (Urrieta, 2004b).

People of color in various communities continue to use such sayings as put-downs. We must stop and analyze what this means because even when we jokingly make fun of ourselves, something is implied in this type of language. In an interview conducted with a young Chicano student in 2001, in reference to this topic, he said:

> People are afraid of who they are [his emphasis]. People are afraid of speaking Spanish because they feel they're gonna be called on it—either they're going to be looked down upon as one of "them" or because there's people who always wanna put a standard on how to speak Spanish, and how you should act, you know? It's a sad thing because it happens a lot in our community....I would say it's like what Frantz Fanon says in *Wretched of the Earth*. It's like the colonized person wants to be like the colonizer. And it's true. And the thing is that you always wanna fight being divided and conquered.

Part of this fear of bilingual education, or of mixing Spanish-speaking children with English-speaking children, or developing biliteracy simultaneously (such as by language mixing), in part comes from this fear of ourselves—of our own internalized oppression; of our painful experience with whitestreaming.

Whitestreaming hurts! Internalized oppression hurts the people whom we learn to fear, and/or hate, and it also hurts us. Internalized oppression, like racism, hurts White people just as much as it hurts people of color, they just do not know it. The unfortunate side about both internalized oppression and racism is that we all lose out on incredible opportunities to learn from each other. The altruistic sense in bridging different linguistic communities is lost (Soto, 2002a).

WHAT IT TAKES

For any bilingual program to work it is vital and necessary that an educator have a positive attitude and believe in what he/she is doing. I do not mean believing así más o menos, I mean believing con todo el corazón that what you are doing is right. Teaching is an act of love and teaching students bilingually is no exception. I learned to be patient with my students and to understand the context in which they were learning. U.S.-born Latinas/os are in an optimal position to do that because, unlike language purists, we have lived the simultaneously bilingual linguistic context our students experience.

I have learned that when students mix languages it is not a linguistic sin, rather an opportunity to develop multilingual competencies. Simultaneous bilinguals use language in optimal ways. This intricate use of languages creates a distinct and highly complex use of language. If, as educators, we only better tapped into these linguistic resources instead of punishing students for mixing languages, we might be making better progress. If whitestream teachers stopped looking at language mixing as a deficit instead of a resource, educators could design lessons that look at individual students' language patterns and design lessons on how to effectively teach bidirectionally—either Spanish or English language skills—based on each student's strengths and use of language (Dworin, 2003).

Believing in what you do as a bilingual educator and believing in your students are of utmost importance. Every student is intelligent, an inherently good person, and most parents of bilingual students care about their children and their education. If you do not believe in what you are doing as a bilingual teacher and in the potential and abundance of knowledge your students and their families possess, then you do not have hope, esperanza. Being a bilingual teacher requires having esperanza; there is no set path to making every program work in the same way because whitestream society has not allowed bilingual programs to ever fully flourish unless they benefit English speakers in some way.

We need to move away from the consumerist thought, namely that in order to see progress in a bilingual program it must meet high program performance measures evidenced by annual multiple choice exams devised by whitestreamed assessment procedures. These types of program assessments do not accurately demonstrate quality teaching. Sometimes the fruits of your work are not readily apparent because it takes a certain kind of person to do this kind of work, the kind of work that in order to be effective regardless of what kinds of students you work with requires faith and esperanza for a better tomorrow. El tipo de trabajo de un/a maestra/o bilingüe es aquel que si lo hacemos con ganas, con esperanza, y con fe, nunca nos vamos a dar por vencidos, siempre vamos a estar alegres, y nunca morirá la esperanza de ver un futuro mejor (Urrieta, 2004a).

One of my first tasks upon returning from the summer 1997 seminar on critical pedagogy was to stop eating lunch in the teacher lunchroom. Unfortunately, the teacher lunchroom, where I worked, was a place filled with poison and with negativity. I made it a point to surround myself with positive people, people who were always trying to be optimistic even during the hard times. Instead, I joined groups of bilingual teachers that had writer's workshops, we shared lesson plans and our successes as well as our struggles. Networks of support to counterbalance the negativity of the whitestream toward bilingual education, bilingual teachers, bilingual students and their families are very important in the struggle to make bilingual programs work.

THE CULTURAL TREASURES OF LANGUAGE

When I realized that I had as much to learn from my students as they had from me, I began to use cultural language projects in my classes. With these projects students began to collect cuentos (stories), dichos (sayings), regaños (scolding), recetas (recipes), oraciones (prayers), and consejos (advice) from their parents, grandparents, tias y tios, and other community members. Community knowledge was at the core of the activities. It was also then that I became more and more reaffirmed in my practices as a bilingual teacher because I realized that so much of who we are as cultural beings is contained in language (Gonzalez, 2005). It became clear to me that the whitestreaming process is indeed a process of cultural genocide that must be battled/combated.

My students would come back with treasure chests (figuratively speaking) of cuentos y dichos, recipes, and prayers they collected. I rarely had students not do their homework. The students were excited about what they were doing because it was relevant to their and their family's experience. Below are some examples of these dichos:

- *Camaron que se Duerme se lo lleva la corriente*
- *No hay mal que por bien no venga*
- *Quien mucho abarca poco aprieta*

- *Ojos que no ven corazon que no siente*

And the list went on and on until over my last two years as a teacher I collected over 150 dichos. My students also collected canciones y rimas:

- *Brinca la tablita yo ya la brinque, brincala otra vuelta que ya me canse*

And the infamous rima a lot of us heard as children whenever we got hurt:

- *Sana, sana, colita de rana si no sanas hoy sanaras mañana*

It was amazing to see my students and their families so excited about schoolwork!

As a bilingual teacher, I realized that when we lose our language, we lose a fundamental part of who we are. It sometimes saddens me that some people in our community even lose their ability to communicate with their own families. I know some who have never been able to have a meaningful conversation with their grandparents. I ask myself, how much knowledge is lost with a generation when a language dies with it? Language is intricately linked to cultural identity, part of ourselves dies when we lose our language, it's a matter of cultural genocide. Subsequently, we learn to devalue ourselves when our language and our people are devalued.

CONCLUDING THOUGHTS

Any one of us can be an oppressor by subscribing uncritically to enforcing the tenets of whitestreaming, including through linguicism. As bell hooks (1994) writes, it is not the English language that hurts but how the oppressors use it—how it used to exclude, humiliate, and punish. A well-prepared and dedicated bilingual teacher can help to liberate bilingual students from the oppressive whitestreaming process and help students achieve their full linguistic potential. Bilingual teachers can help combat the negative views and low expectations the whitestream has of Latina/o students, especially Mexican Americans and Puerto Rican Americans.

Teachers are powerful role models for their students. Students still look up to them—especially if teachers believe in their potential, if they respect them and their families, and they love them. Students will rise to teachers' expectations. When teachers have low expectations, students learn quickly that only a little effort is required to make their teachers happy. El trabajo de un/a maestra/o bilingüe si se hace con ganas, con esperanza, y con fe, nunca se daran por vencidos, siempre estaran alegres, y nunca morira la esperanza de ver un futuro mejor para sus alumnos.

Bilingual teachers should pursue the ideals of this great nation for their students—life, liberty, and the pursuit of happiness—without exceptions!. This country was founded on the proposition of equality. I say proposition because I do not yet believe equality has been achieved. Rather, teachers continue to struggle in their pursuit of quality bilingual education. Bilingual teachers are working to give their students a chance to excel and, at the same time, are nourishing the global citizens of tomorrow. Bilingual teachers are bold to take on the challenge of modeling bilingual education and supporting bilingual programs—this is the crux of global citizenship and equality. There is no room for passivity or questioning in bilingual education as selected players have done. Rather, we must continue to push the boundaries and do what is right for the most vulnerable of all our people.

CHAPTER SIX

Puertorriqueña como yo

MARIA R. SCHARRÓN-DEL RÍO

All people have a basic need to share stories.

(KOKI, 1998, P.1)

My mother is a storyteller. Had she been born in another time or culture, she would have been groomed in the oral history traditions of her group and would have had the task of passing it on to the next generations. She would have also been a medicine woman, but that's another story. As it turned out, growing up within Puerto Rico in the second half of the 20th century, her calling took the form of being a teacher.

I was two years old, my mother recalls, when I first claimed my place among storytellers in the family. As one of the youngest in my extended family reunions, I would drag my much older cousins to sit on the ground in a semicircle and I would tell them stories. I would repeat the stories I had heard from my mother and from small 45 RPM recorded read-along storybooks. I played them on a handed down child record player, which at other times doubled as carousel for my Fisher Price toys.

At two, when faced with a potentially overwhelming event, such as a multitude of people much taller and older than me, I found a way to engage and influence them through storytelling. The structured activity of storytelling helped me to find my voice and to figure out a comfortable place for myself within my family. Why did I choose to tell stories? Although I cannot remember that first time, I believe that I chose to tell stories because I enjoyed them; because I had experienced, first-hand, the power of storytelling through my mother.

To this day, whenever my mother tells a story, her face lights up and her whole demeanor shifts. She becomes ageless and light. I have more recently noticed how, while she is telling her stories, my breathing slows, my muscles relax, and everything else disappears, but her. I look back to my childhood and realize I have experienced this reaction to her stories since a very early age. Moreover, I generalized this relaxation response to other forms and instances of storytelling—reading, studying, and the classroom. I would argue that this response may also be experienced in other cultures as well, seeing how prevalent bedtime stories are, and how many of us, as adults, like to engage in reading as a way to settle down for bed.

Storytelling occurs across cultures, but it remains particularly significant for many cultural, ethnic, and linguistic minorities: Indigenous (Native), Latino/a, of African descent, and of Asian/Pacific Islander descent. Its intersections with cultural/ethnic/racial identity are multiple and complex. It is used as a means to entertain, as a vehicle for preserving history and tradition, as a culturally sensitive research method for indigenous people, as a mode of inquiry (both self and communal), as pedagogy (from literacy to mathematics to social sciences), and as an intervention (both individual and community oriented). Nevertheless, since it has not been a part of the dominant cultural paradigm in the United States, its use in bilingual and regular education has been usually limited to literacy efforts (Anzaldúa, 1999; Begay, 2002; Burk, 2000; Carter-Black, 2007; Cowell, 2002; Koki, 1998).

LANGUAGE AND LEARNING

Mothers (and other primary attachment figures) are, as the cliché goes, our first teachers. Nevertheless, this role of first educator is not dictated by gender or genealogical closeness. Anyone who becomes the primary attachment figure of a child becomes by default his or her first teacher. That my mother is an educator by vocation only magnified her influence in my academic, language, cognitive, and identity development. By frequently talking, reading, and telling me stories, she provided a very rich environment and enhanced my language development.

Everything and every time were good for a story. Outings to the grocery store could include stories about buildings that used to be on the way to the store and now were gone. This could lead to a narrative about the economic changes that Puerto Rico had endured in the last century. And most of the time, it included a reference to my mother's life. This made history real, significant, pertinent, and alive. Things are much easier to learn in context than in a vacuum.

Her stories were about not only providing me with information, but also help-ing me to develop buen juicio (good judgment). Anzaldúa (1999) talks about sto-ries that are meant to protect. Many stories gave me reasons to do things and not to do things. Any warning or caution imparted by my mother, grandmother, or other elders in my family usually came with a story about terrible consequences "M'ija, no jueges bola en la calle. Mira que el otro día vino un carro y pisó a un nene en la calle de al lado. Está vivo de milagro." Stories about kids my age (they were usual-ly my age, regardless how old I was when the story was told) suffering bodily harm due to poor judgment, disobedience, or the evil nature of humankind were common in the daily conversations.

My introduction to English, as many bilingual children experience, came through school. English was the only subject in which my mother did not feel com-fortable helping me during the later part of my grade school years. My mother still refrains from speaking English, although she can understand it well. Her insecu-rity stems from having done all her schooling with Spanish Catholic nuns. English was not emphasized in her school in Puerto Rico. She can read and write it, but sel-dom ventures to speak in English during a conversation with an English speaker. This came as a surprise to the teachers and school administration of the Catholic grade school I attended in Puerto Rico. The school was run by U.S. nuns from Philadelphia, and many of the classes were taught in English.

My mother often tells of the time that the school psychologist engaged her in conversation. The school psychologist was a U.S.-born-and-raised White woman, and although we were in Puerto Rico, she greeted my mother and began talking with her in English. After a while, she asked my mother a question, and my mother answered in Spanish. The psychologist was surprised to learn that neither of my par-ents spoke English at home. My mother usually ends the story saying that she had told the psychologist that she had nothing to do with my English proficiency—that it was a product of the school and my own interest.

My mother may not have taught me English, but I believe she provided me with everything I needed to learn it—the means (general language skills) and the medi-um (storytelling). Storytelling gave the structure upon which my language skills developed. Since I loved stories, and my mother often read to me from various books, I had an interest and urgency to learn to read. Once I learned to read, I would devour books and stories incessantly. Many of my English teachers had small libraries of books in English within the classroom. Learning to read in English also became very important, as it expanded the number of sources I could go to for more stories. Eventually, having access to literature in both English and Spanish helped me to make sense of the complicated maze of being bicultural.

Ethnic Identity Is Twin Skin to Linguistic Identity

Ser y no querer ser…es la divisa (de Burgos, 1982)[1]

—I AM MY LANGUAGE (ANZALDÚA, 1999, P. 81)

Telling stories always involves relating to something that transcends us. Stories emerge from our interaction with something (i.e., the universe) or someone else. The process of narrating stories implies reflecting on our experiences—either because we seek to retrieve the story from the memory of when we first heard it or because we have been witness to the events that it attempts to describe. If the story comes from our internal experience, it is about our relationship with the outside world shaping our inner world. If it alludes to an outside event, it has been filtered through our senses and the narrative is constructed according to our past stories as well. Whatever we choose to share, it remains our interpretation of what we have witnessed or heard. This reflexive and dynamic quality of stories enables them to be shaped and reshaped as we narrate them, listen to them, and retell them. It also enables us to change our interpretations of the events as we explore and revisit what happened and think about what could have been different (Koki, 1998; Stern, 1985).

This dynamic quality of stories is particularly significant in our process of constructing, deconstructing, and reconstructing our identities. It also helps us organize our experiences as we record important experiences. As I was growing up bilingual and bicultural, knowing about my past, my ancestry, and my country's history gave me solid ground upon which I built my own story. These cimientos (foundation) gave me a sense of belonging and purpose that helped me make sense of my particular challenges and struggles (Koki, 1998).

This knowledge I also owe to my mother's stories. I know a lot of my mother's life because she chose to share it in her narratives. I learned early on about my country's struggles and changes because they were part of my mother's accounts. My mother conveyed her coming of age and her finding a purpose in her life through her stories. She provided me with examples of how a young Puerto Rican woman, like me, had been able to challenge the status quo. I was able to identify with her and later differentiate from her, thanks to these narratives. I learned who she was and inferred whom she wanted me to become through her stories.

I was able to fit my own life story into the web of stories that my mother and her ancestors had woven before me. I saw myself as the child of two progressive Puerto Ricans, who were able to separate from their families' oppressive and/or limiting conditions and fight for their personal and their country's freedom. I was able to see my lineage in being part of the resistance, of those committed to equality, social change, and justice. Both my parents, and particularly my mother, took strong stances against the status quo and were respected for it. I embraced my place as an agent of change in my country's struggle for self-determination, equal rights, and freedom. I rebelled and resisted against my personal instances of oppression. I was able to start making peace with the paradoxes and contradictions that the half a millennium of colonial rule has branded onto my country's daily life.

THE POWER OF LEARNING TO LISTEN AND BEING LISTENED TO

Bilingual and bicultural children often struggle with the conflicts that living in and between worlds and worldviews suppose. When one language is favored over another, a world is valued over another. Linguistic instruction is never devoid of cultural and ethnic messages. To think or believe otherwise is to perpetuate the discourse of oppression and value differences that society explicitly and implicitly conveys. Similarly, to assume language instruction as culture-neutral is to perpetuate linguistic privilege.

Bilingual and bicultural children, as part of a minority in an oppressive society, are keenly aware of and extremely sensitive to the messages that mainstream society conveys about their "other" language and culture. These messages can become threatening enough to silence their voices. In my work as a child psychologist, I have been referred children who upon entering Head Start or preschool have become silent. The clinical term for such a behavior is selective mutism.

Miguel[2] was five years old when I first saw him. His teacher, doctor, and mother were concerned because he would not speak to anyone at school. He had started kindergarten several months before, and he still would not speak. His mother told me that when she asked him why he would not talk at school he said it was because he did not know how to speak English. He was the second child in a Latino family that had immigrated to a large urban community. His mother had been an educator-in-training in her country of origin when she first decided to come to the United States. She provided a rich environment for Miguel and his older sibling, frequently reading to them in Spanish. When it was time for Miguel to begin his schooling, she had been counseled by the school administration to enroll him in a monolingual classroom.

When I first saw Miguel, no one besides his family had heard him talk—yet his mother reported that he had a very large vocabulary in Spanish and spoke incessantly at home. Initially, Miguel did not speak with me, although he was able to answer yes/no questions by nodding and concrete choice questions by pointing. He would play quietly with little figures and engage in coloring with pencils and crayons. I introduced myself in Spanish to Miguel, and asked him if he wanted me to talk to him in Spanish (he nodded).

I found out that he loved stories. His mother told me that he would make series of drawings at home and staple them together as stories. I began printing out volumes of coloring pages, and he would choose the ones he liked and we would spend time coloring them and putting them together. I would ask him questions about the stories he was building, and by the end of the first month, he began to answer some of my questions by mouthing words. After three months of meeting with him, Miguel began speaking to me in a whisper-like voice. I believe that by finding a nonjudgmental person outside of his family that was interested in his stories, the love and desire he had to share them helped him brave the fear of exposing his "voice."

Finding your voice as a bilingual child can be scary, confusing, and frightening. All of the conflicts between the values and worldviews of the languages involved weigh heavily upon us. You want to remain loyal to your cultural heritage while being painfully sensitive to the costs of doing so. At the same time, you want to belong, to be part of the privileged culture. You want to play during recess and not be made fun of. You want to feel powerful, and this comes through acceptance and validation by the systems that surround you.

For Miguel, these conflicts took away his voice; he became publicly ashamed of it. He had to regain confidence in his voice in order to speak out. Anzaldúa (1999) refers to overcoming similar struggles when she says, "I will no longer be made to feel ashamed of existing...I will overcome the tradition of silence" (p. 81).

When Miguel began mouthing and whispering to me, all of his answers were in English. At times, he would not answer my question if he did not know how to say it in English. He had internalized the social request that outside of the family he was only supposed to talk in English. To talk in Spanish with people that he did not know was exposing himself to the possibility of rejection and ridicule. Nevertheless, he preferred that I spoke Spanish in our meetings. Listening to me talk Spanish was reassuring, comforting, and safe. It conveyed that I valued that part of him that others seemed to threaten and mock.

I once was able to hear him talk to his mother in Spanish. I was walking home from work and ran into Miguel and his mother on the street. Miguel did not see me, but his mother did. She smiled and asked Miguel about his day at school. She wanted me to hear him as she heard him. What followed was a rich and elaborated account, in Spanish, of his classes, his newfound friends, the new topics he was learning...So many stories! I was extremely moved and honored by Miguel's mom's gesture, as it had truly been a gift. She enabled me to witness and listen to Miguel's voice expressing confidently in a way that I had sensed but was still struggling to hear. That voice was the one that various school administrators and teachers had devalued, questioned, and silenced. It was the voice of his "otherness."

I suggested to his mother that she request Miguel be transferred to a bilingual classroom within the same school. The school was reluctant to make the change, and he spent the first semester of his first grade in a monolingual classroom again. During that first month, Miguel continued his silence in school. When asked about his classmates, he would say that he had no friends at school and that everyone was "mean." Finally, he was transferred to a bilingual classroom, and to the administration's surprise, that very same day Miguel was "whispering" to the teacher and trying to engage and play with other children. Slowly, he began to develop appropriate relationships with his classmates. He was still shy in class, but he often communicated with his teacher and enjoyed school.

Creating Linguistically Safe Spaces

It is a great challenge to genuinely foster the development of skills and knowledge in two languages when our society and institutions offer constant and consistent messages about which one is "better." Making space for cultural narratives within the classroom is a way to start validating other ways of acquiring and disseminating knowledge. By bringing into the classroom stories, sayings, riddles, rhymes, and songs from the students' ethnic cultures we challenge the notion that subjugates one language/culture under another.

García and Bartlett (2007) describe several elements that help create a linguistically safe space within bilingual education. In their description of a highly successful New York City high school that targets English as a second language acquisition in Latino/a newcomers, García and Bartlett attribute the success to its vision of "second language acquisition as a social process building on the speech community itself" (p.1). With this vision, educators create a safe space in which the students can feel at ease while learning and experimenting linguistically. This is of utmost importance. García and Bartlett (2007) also identified one of the characteristics that contributed to the creation of this linguistically safe space as the high status of Spanish within the speech community of the high school. They argue that since English monolingualism was not implicitly or explicitly the norm, the students' Spanish language identity was protected and valued. With their language identity unthreatened, English and Spanish were more equal in the eyes of the students.

Additionally, García and Bartlett report that this school used bilingualism as a pedagogical tool. Students wrote and shared autobiographical narratives in their Language Arts classes. Most teachers were bilingual and shared with students sayings, humor, and stories similar to their own. These practices allowed the students to use their language of origin to connect deeply with the members of their speech community—another instance that contributed to creating a trusting and safe space.

USING CULTURALLY RELEVANT NARRATIVES IN BILINGUAL EDUCATION

My younger sister, like my mother, is also a teacher. She has attended various conferences on Lecto Escritura (Reading and Writing Instruction) in Guatemala and Panamá. She has visited various grade schools during her stay in both countries. As I shared with her part of my research for this chapter, she mentioned that she had seen various instances of storytelling in the classroom throughout her visit to both countries. She mentioned that in one classroom, the teachers would dress up and become cuentacuentos; they transformed themselves into storytellers for part of the lesson. Cuentacuentos were part of their cultural tradition.

As teachers, there are many ways in which we may incorporate stories and other cultural narratives in the classroom. Here are a few suggestions:

1. Get acquainted with your students' culture—All ethnic and cultural groups have traditional narrative practices; some of them unique. Search to expand your knowledge about your students' ethnicities and cultures.

2. Include a time for narratives in the lesson plan—Have your students ask their family members about stories, sayings, riddles, rhymes, tongue twisters, and songs from their ethnic background that pertain to one of the day's topics.

3. Invite family members to share their narratives in the classroom—Invite parents and grandparents to the classroom to tell stories and engage with the students in their first language.

4. Incorporate autobiographical storytelling as a pedagogical tool—Help students engage in telling their life stories as a way to share struggles, explore conflicts, develop empathy, and understand themselves in relation to others.

5. Listen actively and sensitively—Communicate interest in their stories and be sensitive to the conflicts and struggles that come from living between and within two cultures. Be aware of your values and how they may be similar to or different from your students.

6. Communicate high regard and respect toward different ways of communicating and seeing the world—Showing respect toward the students' native language and culture helps create a linguistically safe space that promotes not only language development but also emotional well-being.

SUMMARY

Throughout this chapter, I have advocated the use of storytelling along with other cultural narrative practices (i.e., use of sayings, rhymes, riddles, and songs) as part of a holistic and culturally competent approach while teaching bilingual/bicultural children. I have argued that developing in an environment rich in cultural narrative practices fosters language and cognitive skills, academic success, and the development of children's identity on many levels (i.e., language, ethnic, cultural, racial). Stimulating and validating children's stories in both languages will help them find and honor their own voices.

Notes

1. "To be and not want to be…that's the motto"–English translation from *Song of the Simple Truth: Obra Poética Completa—The Complete Poems of Julia de Burgos*, compiled and translated by Jack Agüeros (de Burgos & Agüeros, 1997).
2. Names and identifying information have been changed and/or altered to protect the privacy and confidentiality of those included.

Critical Analyses

Los Consejos

CHAPTER SEVEN

Race Matters for Bilingual/Bicultural Children

DELIDA SANCHEZ

Mrs. Rose is Irish American of working-class background and is the first in her family to obtain a master's degree. She has been teaching in a second grade Brooklyn classroom for 4 years and loves her job. She is committed to giving back to other students from similar socioeconomic backgrounds. She is well liked by her diverse student class and is known for going "above and beyond the call of duty" in her interaction with students. Her class is comprised mostly of Russian/Eastern European, Irish American, Chinese American, Black, Latino/a and a few Italian American, Jewish American children. She is a proud "product" of the New York City School System.

> Ms. Penny and Mrs. Rose went to college together and attended the same master's program for teaching. Ms. Penny is a white Spanish teacher from an upper middle class family who has traveled a great deal and has been involved as a volunteer in Latin America and Spain. Mrs. Rose invited Ms. Penny for "Hispanic Heritage Week."
>
> Luci is a bright, energetic, friendly, 7-year-old Puerto Rican student, who was very excited about "Hispanic Heritage Week." Luci, who is sometimes called derogatory names because of her hair texture and skin color, looked forward to "proving her authenticity" and to celebrate her heritage.
>
> Mrs. Rose: "Does anyone know how to say father/daddy in Spanish?"
> Luci: "I know..." (quickly raises her hand and proudly says) "Papi"
> Mrs. Rose: "I'm sorry Luci, that's incorrect. The Spanish word for father is papa."
> Luci: "But that is what I call my father."

Luci appears confused, when she adds, "Papi is what my mother and father taught me to call my daddy."

Mrs. Rose assumed Luci was African American and asks, "Where is your family from?"

Luci: "My family is from Puerto Rico."

Mrs. Rose: "Oh, well, that explains it. Puerto Ricans speak a Spanish slang." Mrs. Rose maintains that Puerto Ricans' and Dominicans' "ways of Speaking Spanish" makes it difficult for her to understand them. She is often irritated and is intent on imposing "Castillian Spanish" with 'correct' grammatical structures (in spite of it being a completely different dialect/language and sociocultural context for the children).

Mrs. Rose did not understand that her efforts to "help" Luci by judging/qualifying her use of Spanish language would have negative consequences on her ethnic/cultural identity development. Less obvious is the oversight of Luci's racial development.which could be further damage her ethnic and cultural identity. It is even possible that this could lead to to confusion and internalized racism.

RACE MATTERS TO ME

As a Latina bilingual/ bicultural New York City psychologist, educator and "survivor" of the public school system, racial development has been an important aspect in my evolution personally and professionally as well as for the urban youth that I work with. My current passion and work among bilingual/ bicultural populations stems from a long history of being racially misrepresented and misunderstood. Addressing the classroom is often fraught with anxiety, fear, frustration, and anger. I often say to myself, "I hate talking about race. I wish it didn't matter." But it does. As the population of Latinos/as and Asians continues to grow rapidly, addressing race within and without the Black-White racial binary is very important.

I'm asked by White colleagues in academia and the school system, for solutions to complex racial problems affecting bilingual/bicultural youth. I feel that I am doomed to fail because our children do not fall into neat categories. There is an expectation that we have "arrived" at racial equality. It seems as if only persons of color can solve the racism that exists in schools. I often feel burdened by this unfair expectation.

You're so cute I'm gonna call you "little monkey" with your short curly hair and beige face from now on," my friend and classmate decided one day. I was stunned. I knew my friend didn't mean harm but the comment was upsetting and left me feeling reduced/self-conscious. I really look like a monkey? I began to want to emulate the healing qualities of the "care bears" (translated in Spanish to little monkey) and began to sing and dance in our living room at home thinking perhaps that was the intention. But then I also remember being called a variety of names that were racially derogatory, like nigger. I did not want to be associated with the term as other class-mates began to sing the care bear commercial in Spanish. They would sing the jin-gle over and over. "You're not Puerto Rican you are Black!" I found myself defending my Puerto Rican African American ethnic/cultural identity.

It was only after attending college and learning about the racial history of Puerto Rican that I began to understand on my skin color. Previous to these experiences there had been an invisibility to my identity since people could not put me in a 'neat category' of racial identity. My story represents the history of a whole group of peo-ple who have been colonized, enslaved, and misunderstood.

RACE MATTERS IN THE CLASSROOM

The opening scenario and aforementioned recollection of my experiences as a child can help to demonstrate how race is important for teachers to consider when work-ing with children. Teachers can confuse children's identities by misunderstanding the child's background, the family's culture, the home language, and physical fea-tures. Teacher behaviors can cause additional stressors by expecting total assimila-tion and acculturation in school. The story of Luci does not only apply to Latinos but also other bilingual/bicultural racial groups such as Asians. I have seen Chinese students being mistaken for Korean or Japanese (and vice versa). Asian children can also be tormented by being called "chinaman," "chink," and "ching chong," among others. These terms can have long lasting effects on children's identity and cultur-al development.

Bilingual/ bicultural students do not fit easily into the prevailing United Statian racial categories. They also share unique physical attributes that make them not read-ily identifiable. The skin color may vary, their facial features may be unique, they may have White skin with blue eyes, or Black skin with green eyes, etc. Understanding these nuances is key for teachers, since there are complex sociocul-tural elements involved such as the child's country of origin, migratory patterns, common ancestry, language, culture, history, and traditions. These are all key ele-ments for racial understandings.

TEACHER AWARENESS OF RACE WITH BILINGUAL/BICULTURAL STUDENTS

Too many teacher education programs ignore current research about how bilingual/ bicultural children develop racial identity and attitudes. Discussions are often cen-tered on the White American perspectives. The racial experiences bilingual/ bicultural groups are often omitted or subsumed under discussions about immigration and acculturation. As a result many teachers, the majority of whom are White, address the issues in superficial and simplistic ways. Examples of the latter include putting up posters during multicultural week, asking children to bring dishes that represent their ethnic/cultural group, and sharing their culture during "show and tell." There is no systemic incorporation of the racial histories of most ethnic groups in history books, reading material, and other educational tools for learning. The denial of this information means that children can be taught contradictory information and bias.

THE DEVELOPMENT OF RACE AMONG BILINGUAL/BICULTURAL CHILDREN

Race is not an abstraction to young children. By age 3 there is already an awareness of race. Children are made aware of their skin color, hair texture, facial features, etc.in society by television, magazines, books and family members. They are also made aware of privileges associated with being light/white. In elementary school and beyond, students learn that White students have access to preferential treatment by teachers, entry into good schools, and popularity among one's peers. Moreover, children of all races express a preference for white dolls and use white colors to portray themselves in pictures and drawings. By age 5 children of color have already begun to internalize negative images of themselves (Clark & Clark, 1939: Cross, 1991: Derman-Sparks, 1985).

STRATEGIES FOR ADDRESSING RACE ON BEHALF OF BILINGUAL/BICULTURAL CHILDREN

The following recommendations may prove useful for teachers working with bilingual/bicultural children:

- Include authentic and accurate racial diversity experiences and discussions.
- Help to hire and support a knowledgeable and compassionate bilingual/bicultural teaching staff.
- Teach the importance of affirming and respecting diversity.

CHAPTER EIGHT

Mi Pobre Guerito

OCTAVIO PIMENTEL

As a critical, Chicano professor, I understand the politics of Mexican American parents not teaching their children Spanish. I understand that racism and linguicism against Brown, Spanish-speaking individuals is alive and well, making the choice to teach Spanish to our children difficult. In the United States the Spanish language is often commonly associated with a demonized Mexican national identity. Since many Mexican American parents have experienced this racism and linguicism themselves, they often do not want their children to relive these experiences—thus choosing not to teach their children Spanish. The hope is that by not teaching their children Spanish, they will be classified as "American" and not as part of an ethnic culture. Ironically, this rarely happens. Although there are various reasons why this does not happen, one explanation is that some people often confuse American with Aryan characteristics, thus systematically excluding American people of color from being able to possess an "American national identity"—Spanish-speaking or not. Despite the difficulties that Spanish-speaking individuals face in this country, I have decided to teach my children Spanish. In this chapter, I analyze how my son's language identity, Spanish monolingual, has been perceived as he begins his educational journey in a pre-kindegarten bilingual program.

At a glance, my family may seem as a typical bilingual couple with three children, who live in a middle-class neighborhood. The truth is that we are much more complicated than that. Yo soy Mexicano. My parents are from Michoacán and

Jalisco, and I was born in Califas. I grew up as a migrant worker. Our family traveled from Texas all the way to Washington state, picking whatever fruit was in season. Spanish was my first language and I did not learn English until much later. My parents always taught me to be extremely proud of my Mexican culture and my Spanish language. Simply said, Soy frijolero, con el nopal en la frente¡

My wife Charise is different. Although I do consider her bilingual/bicultural, she is of the White race. She is a beautiful, six-foot tall blonde woman, with light skin and blue eyes—her ancestry rooted in Welch and German culture. On the inside, o como se dice en español—en el corazón—Charise is Mexicana. Even though she has been speaking Spanish for over 25 years, and still has an English accent, she has faced and overcome many of the obstacles Brown Spanish-speaking individuals have faced.

While growing up, Charise lived in "Hollywood," a placaso for a dangerous Mexican barrio. Since my suegra was a single mother and suffered from anxiety attacks, she could not work; thus she and her two kids were extremely poor. Up until Charise was old enough to work, her mother bought her two pairs of pants, three shirts, and one pair of shoes to last her an entire year. In hopes of helping her, the migrant families often gave Charise their old clothes.

Our unique histories/herstories emphasized one thing: cultural pride. We both grew up learning not to be ashamed of where we came from, but rather to be proud of it. Consequently, we both recognized the importance of Mexican American cultural practices, including speaking Spanish. With this in mind, Charise and I named our first child Quetzin Luis Pimentel. The name "Quetzin" is nahuatl and it means Aztec leader. "Luis" is the name of my deceased father who overcame many racist obstacles in the United States to become a successful business person. Pimentel is the name carried from my family for over several generations.

Physically, Quetzin looks White. He has green eyes and is light complected—but with the ability to tan easily. He has a slender build with extremely long arms and legs. Wanting Quetzin to be bilingual, Charise and I decided to teach/speak only Spanish to him. Specifically, this means that 100% of our communication to him, as well as all the other language sources provided in our home including toys, DVDs, games, books, and playmates, are Spanish.

After living in Texas for a year, Quetzin was old enough to attend a bilingual pre-kindergarten (pre-k) program. The pre-k program in our district targets at-risk students—those students who are also typically identified as low-income and/or language minority students (e.g., Spanish monolingual speakers). Since Quetzin is a monolingual Spanish speaker, the school identified him as an at-risk student and thus he qualified for the program. The irony of this is that Quetzin is anything but at-risk. He has been reading since age four.

By November, Ms. Baiza (Quetzin's teacher) informed us that Quetzin was a very advanced student. For example, pre-K students are expected to count to 10 and know the alphabet by the end of the academic school year. By November, Quetzin was counting to 30 and could recite the entire alphabet as well as all of the sonidos. In addition, he could also spell and write his name, his two sisters' names, as well as his parents' names. The only problem he had was with cutting, which was attributed to his big hands and his inability to use ordinary child-sized scissors.

After Christmas break, and an extended stay in California, Quetzin returned to school. The afternoon of his first day back from school, Quetzin came home with a brown grocery bag, filled with various items, none of which were wrapped, and a note indicating that an older child from the school had donated this gift for Christmas. In the bag, there were soap, toothpaste, a toothbrush, some used toys and books. Somehow, it had been decided that my child was considered financially needy, and thus was adopted by a more affluent (likely a White) family. Apparently, Quetzin's "at-risk" language status engulfed his entire being. That is, he was no longer only at-risk because of his language, but for any number of other factors, including his perceived socio-economic status.

My first intentions were to return the bag, meet with the teacher, principal, and district school superintendent, and to call them out on their racist ideologies and practices. While designing my plan, I talked to my son about it and he told me not to do anything. As he smiled, he told me that he was happy with his gifts. With his reassurance, I calmed down and did not pursue this problem further.

The experience that my family went through is not unique. This kind of deficit labeling commonly happens to Mexican American bilingual students across the nation. In many schools, bilingual education programs are marginalized within the larger school, often understood as programs that meet students' "special needs"— providing instruction in minority languages in the interim of students learning English, at which point they can be mainstreamed in "normal" classrooms. Because of the deficit status that is attached to bilingual programs and their students, it is difficult for the larger schools to conceptualize bilingual students outside of deficit terms. As was the case in Quetzin's experience, the school could not conceive of ways for older White children to interact with younger bilingual students outside of these deficit conceptions. In Quetzin's school, the teachers and students set up a program that allowed more affluent (more often than not) White students to donate materials to the bilingual education students. Although in theory this may sound like a good practice, this is a racist practice because bilingual students are being marginalized because of their first language as well as their perceived socio-economic status (which is often based on their language status).

Schools need to be aware of the implications of these practices. The practice of "adopting" a bilingual child puts that child in a subordinate and patronizing position, while reinforcing the idea that the adoptive family (usually White) is dominant and can be helpful to minority students. This impacts the bilingual child's self-esteem because although he/she may not understand the complexity compounded by social issues that include race, ethnicity, and socio-economic status, in many cases he/she recognizes that he/she is Brown and is being "helped" by a White family. Moreover, White English-speaking children and their families learn that they are model students who are in the position of helping those in need, thus reinforcing their already privileged status.

These unequal practices can often negatively affect the Spanish-speaking children who do need financial assistance. There are other ways to provide assistance that do not work from the traditional assumptions based on race, language, and need. Perhaps the most powerful way to do this is by finding more affluent Mexican American Spanish-speaking families who are willing to donate gifts to the students who do need financial assistance. This affords everyone an opportunity to recognize that there are successful Mexican American families. Just as important, it is crucial not to assume that all Brown Spanish-speaking individuals are in need. Perhaps offering this assistance and asking those families interested to apply for this support would be ideal. Following such a protocol would allow the people who want the financial help to receive it.

Los Consejos Para Los Segundos Padres

The advice I give to teachers is simple: be critical and question school practices that classify students of color and/or language minorities as at-risk or needy. I know this is hard because the school system implicitly works from racist ideologies and expects teachers to passively (re)produce these same racist outcomes. For example, the school system expects teachers to label students who are not fluent in English as deficient. An example of this is labels such as Limited English Proficiency (LEP), a term widely used by schools and teachers, which emphasizes what students are lacking instead of what they already know. Schools also expect teachers to implement a predetermined curriculum that centers on Western European English-speaking cultural knowledge. It also expects teachers to participate in rhetoric that positions poor, Brown, non-English speaking students as needy and teaches (especially White teachers) and White English-speaking students that they are the saviors/the more powerful, those who are able to provide the help.

With teachers embedded in the institutional kinds of racism that schools produce, it is difficult to operate outside of this logic. For example, some of the most obvious school practices that reproduce institutional racism are standardized testing and the push for accountability. If students do not perform well on standardized tests, the teacher can be put on probation, which may lead to the teacher losing his/her job. In Queztin's school's case, if for a number of years their students produce low scores on tests, then it is likely the entire school will be put on probation, which may lead to the closure of that school (a Texan probability). High-stakes testing places both teachers and students in vulnerable positions. Students who do not perform well on these tests can be held back a grade, can be assigned mandatory supplemental schooling such as summer school, or can be prohibited from graduating. As a means to identify who needs help passing these national standards, these tests often help guide teachers' practices, such that language and racial minority as well as low income students, whose knowledge is not represented on these tests, are labeled "at-risk" and identified as needing intervention.

As can be seen, these school practices push teachers to decipher who is at-risk or not, based on students' cultural knowledge and native languages. Although these influences/pressures surround teachers, it is crucial for teachers to find ways to displace these forms of institutional racism so they can be more inclusive of all their students' cultural knowledge and languages. For example, teaching units about America's greatest leaders should include non-white people like Dolores Huerta, Reies López Tijerina, and Rodolfo "Corky" Gonzales. Perhaps most important is for teachers to remove themselves from thinking within cultural binaries set up by the school system and to embrace an ideology that welcomes and encourages an interconnected diversity.

Unfortunately, these goals contrast how most teachers have been trained: monolingually and monoculturally. Despite this training, teachers can emphasize the benefits of being bilingual and multicultural. During this process they may point out that the majority of Mexican Americans fully profess the importance of being well-versed in English; however many also recognize the need to maintain fluency in their native Spanish language. Teachers may help produce a new rhetoric claiming that for the future academic it will no longer be good enough to be formally educated in one language, but, instead, the future academic may encompass an overlaying of languages and cultures. Que en el futuro, el academic va ser someone who has the ability and the ganas to switch from one language to the other sin problemas. Asi va ser el academic y ya no más va a ser el English Only academic.

I recognize the consejos I have offered are not easy to follow. The truth is that teachers have been subjected to a rigorous academic training that has taught them that Mexican American Students (and other marginalized groups) are deficient, unmotivated, and lazy and thus are in need of help. Lo que yo los sigo a consejando though is to move away from this deficit way of thinking and to recognize the value Mexican Americans bring to the classroom, which can be done in a variety of ways. For example, in math units it is important for teachers to mention how

Mayans were the founders of "zero." Furthermore, if teachers are teaching a language component, then they can perhaps show an interest and support multiple languages, which would help the teacher gain respect from many of their otherwise marginalized students and parents.

Examining Quetzin's positionality in schools, and bilingual education in particular, is crucial for understanding much of the current deficit models imposed on bilingual and bicultural children. As previously mentioned at the beginning of this chapter, physically my son can be identified as White, but he does not know English and is not familiar with most White cultural practices or mannerisms. In fact, my good friend Estela, a professor in education at a major university in California, and I, commonly find it amusing how her own son, who can easily be identified as Mexican—knows more about White cultural practices than Quetzin.

Quetzin holds a unique position. Because he appears to be White, he will receive many of the privileges allocated to White males. However, because culturally he is also Latino, he will hold multilayered imprints from both cultures.

One of the goals of writing this chapter is to suggest that teachers should not be blamed for their sometimes questionable curriculum or teaching practices. It is important to realize that teachers are heavily guided in curricular and pedagogical practices. It is important for people to recognize that, systematically, the American institution of education is embedded with racist ideology and practice; and thus, only smaller changes can be made until the entire institution acknowledges this problem. Upon this recognition, schools may take larger steps to alleviate systematic racism.

This chapter is written to provide consejos to teachers who play a major role in raising children. Through these consejos, I am optimistic that teachers can recognize their own role in dismantling the racism that systematically exists in the education system, although it may seem they are only taking small steps. It is very important for teachers not to lose faith in the school system despite the various problems it may have. It is important for teachers to recognize that although the changes they make in their classrooms may seem small, they are having a huge impact on the students they serve.

CHAPTER NINE

American Indian[1] Mothers Speaking from the Heart

FRANCES V. RAINS, MELODY BIDTAH, LOVERA BLACK CROW, KARA HORTON & TONI JONES

Between 2002 and 2005, my classroom was the most exciting one of my entire career. I had just left a tenure track position at a flagship university in the Eastern U.S. to have the opportunity to work directly with Native communities in western Washington State, through the Reservation-Based Program at Evergreen State College in Olympia, Washington. As a Choctaw/Cherokee and Japanese woman, it had been my life's dream to work with Native college students.

My inter-tribal college class was held in the Tribal Council Chamber of the Port Gamble S'Klallam Nation in the evening, so as not to conflict with regular Tribal business. The Elwha Klallam students drove over 90 minutes each way to class, the Suquamish students had about a 12 mile drive, and students from other Native Nations (e.g.,Tsimshian, Ojibwe, Nooksack) lived in the vicinity, though, some traveled about 40 miles to class. The Port Gamble S'Klallam students lived close by, so they could drive or walk to class.

My role as the professor was to deliver college-level classes to this Reservation site. I drove two hours each way—bringing books, maps, artwork, lessons and other resources with me. Most of my students were parents—some with small children—who worked all day before attending these night classes, despite the long drives to and from class. Albeit sometimes a bit physically tired (as our classes went until 10 pm), the students were intelligent, dedicated and open to new learning experiences. Still, I had as much to learn from my students, as they had to learn from me.

I worked hard to learn as much as I could about the Coast Salish Nations of the Pacific Northwest (the larger group of Native Nations from which many of the students of my inter-tribal classroom came). I attended their Nations' cultural and community events—especially those of the Port Gamble S'Klallam and Elwha Klallam Nations. Whenever possible, I rolled up my sleeves and helped with whatever jobs I could do. And in the summers, I stayed actively engaged in the communities. I was deeply honored to be given Tribal permission to *pull* (paddle) in the Elwha Klallam Canoes during three separate Tribal Canoe Journeys.

Over time, as my students and I became closer as a learning community, the students shared some of their daily hardships that they, their families, or their Nations were facing (often pertaining to issues of prejudice or racism). We had many discussions about such situations and many of the students, as Native parents and grandparents, consistently raised the concern about the treatment of their children in the local, predominantly white public schools. Wray (2002) writes:

> It is true that Olympic Peninsula tribes are categorized within the Pacific Coast culture because of the general lifestyle elements we share with our neighbors to the north and south: fishing, land and marine hunting, traditional ceremonies, cedar carving, and canoe travel. However, our relationship with the peninsula landscape is unique and distinctive. This relationship spans tens of thousands of years and is based on beliefs and practices tied to specific areas and experiences. Each of the nine tribes….signed treaties between 1854 and 1856 and ceded traditional lands for small reservations. Soon after we were "supervised" on our reservations by missionaries, schoolteachers and Indian agents who set restrictions on passing on our languages and traditions to our children. (pp. xv-xvi)

To some, it may not seem like a big deal to go to a school where the bus drivers, nurses, teachers, coaches, counselors, secretaries and the principal are all white. But imagine that you are just a little Native child from a nearby reservation, and all of a sudden, it can be pretty overwhelming—especially since each of these positions holds some power over your life in school. Compound this with a history of anti-Indian prejudgments and stereotypes, and "overwhelming" no longer seems adequate enough to cover the estrangement, isolation, and disempowerment such circumstances create for Native American children in public schools near Reservations. Thus, this chapter is a brief opportunity to read the perspectives of four Native women as they address two main issues: What would they want teachers to know about Indians? And, what would they want teachers to know about their children?

SPEAKING FROM THE HEART

About the Format

Three choices about this chapter are worthy of discussion here. First, rather than format these women's voices in a traditional academic way—where the professor becomes a ventriloquist (re-telling other peoples' stories, and, thereby, garnering all the credit), the Native mothers and I decided, together, that co-authorship was an empowering and decolonizing way to recognize their contributions. Second, the format for the rest of the chapter is drawn from the style used by Wilma Mankiller (2004), in her book, *Every Day is a Good Day: Reflections by Contemporary Indigenous Women*, where the topic is identified and each woman speaks for herself. Third, as part of the act of reclaiming Indigenous voice and empowerment, each Native woman has chosen to have her real name and identity used.

About the Co-Authors

All of these women were students in my Port Gamble S'Klallam Reservation Site classroom of The Evergreen State College in Olympia, Washington. Each volunteered to share some of their experiences and views as Native parents with children in predominantly white schools near their reservations. Speaking straight from the heart, each hoped their insights might engage those who work in such schools to make a difference for Native American children.

Melody Bidtah, of the Port Gamble S'Klallam Nation, is a mother of three and has earned her Bachelor's Degree. She works for the Port Gamble S'Klallam Tribe. Lovera Black Crow, Elwha Klallam Nation, is the mother of four, and is a junior. She is a stay-at-home mom, who plays softball in Inter-tribal Tournaments. Kara Horton, Port Gamble S'Klallam Nation, is the mother of four children and has earned her Bachelor's Degree. She works for the Port Gamble S'Klallam Tribe and helps with *The S'Klallam View*, a monthly newsletter for the Tribe. And, Toni Jones, Nooksack Nation, is the mother of three and is currently completing her Masters Degree. She works for the Suquamish Tribe. Three of these women went to the same predominantly white schools that their children are now attending, sometimes, with the very same teachers. Here is what they had to say.

What Would You Want Teachers to Know About Indians and Why?

Melody Bidtah

What are teachers learning about Indians *as people*, about Indians *as students?* They just give up on our children. The teachers only teach one way, *their* way. If the Indian kids don't get it the first time, they don't try different strategies. Instead, they think our kids are dumb, and they send them off to Special Education just because they may understand things differently. *It's not right!* Maybe what they need is an Indian

Holocaust Museum so they could learn about us. I went to the Jewish Holocaust Museum in Washington, DC. It was hard, but I learned a lot. Maybe we need an Indian one, so that teachers could learn.

I want teachers to know that children mean *everything* to the Tribe, *everything*, because they are the future. Children are the *joy* of the Tribe. I want teachers to understand how important our children are to us.

Lovera Black Crow

As a child, I was always taught not to look into the eyes of someone who is older than me or someone superior to me, such as my grandma, aunty, or uncle. I was taught that to look someone in the eye was a sign of disrespect toward that person. This mainly applied to situations where I was being told what to do or being disciplined.

In my culture, you are to do as you are told and ask no questions. If I was given an instruction, I was to do just that. You are to take the punishment for your wrong doings without any argument. This can even mean that even if it was not my fault, but my Elder thought it was, I was not to argue with them or correct them. I was simply to submit to my punishment.

I was also taught never to draw attention to myself. I was never to brag about something I had done well. If I did that, I would be dishonoring my upbringing and myself. So as a student, if I knew the answer to a question, I would not raise my hand nor would I blurt out the answer. I would only answer if the teacher called on me. Often Indian children are mistaken to be extremely shy or withdrawn, even possibly dumb, because they do not look their teachers in the eye, they do not raise their hands in class or they have their head down.

When I was in elementary school, I was called upon to answer questions all the time because I never raised my hand or was never actively involved in the class activity. To a teacher, I was just a student who was *obviously* not paying attention or just plainly didn't know the answers.

I feel it is important for teachers to know that Indian children are just as smart as the non-Indian children in their classroom. It is important for every teacher to be educated about the traditional ways of the children they are teaching, and for teachers not to assume an Indian child is unintelligent, or behind, just because of the way they carry themselves.

Kara Horton

Right now, in the public schools here, they don't even mention the Indians from *this* region! The books, and the teachers, seem to have *no clue*! Instead, they teach about the Plains Indians and the Cherokee! When I was a kid, I came home from school thinking *I must be a Cherokee* because those were the *only* Indians our teacher talked about!!! What's weird is, it *hasn't* changed! The teachers *still* do that!!!

The curriculum doesn't tell the truth. It passes on false information. People shouldn't have to wait till college to learn about Indians. People should be able to learn about Indians in K through 12 in a more accurate way! *Things have got to change!* The teachers should be required to learn about Indians. *Everybody* needs to know this, *not just* Indian People—*ALL AMERICANS SHOULD LEARN ABOUT INDIANS.*

I have four children that have gone through the local school district and all were treated the same upon entry of kindergarten. They were placed in what is referred to as the "Assist" program, because they are Native American. It was the assumption that all Native students would do poorly and, therefore, needed extra help from the start. What I learned was that my three sons did need the extra help in learning, however my daughter did not. She was kept in the program through kindergarten and part of her first grade year until her teacher finally realized she did not need the help. Indians are *not* slow learners; they do not need to be stereotyped at such a young age. Yes, appropriate screening should take place and there should be referrals for extra help when necessary. However, lumping students together, especially a minority race, is not key in starting their learning careers on the right path.

Toni Jones

I want teachers to do their research, to do their "homework." That's the most important thing. Teachers need to really know what they are teaching. If a child asks a question about Indians, and the teacher doesn't know the answer, *please don't make up an answer based on the Boy Scouts, the YMCA Indian Guides or something!*

I went into the classroom with one of my daughters, and a little non-Indian boy was sizing us up. He asked, "Where did we get our shoes?" He thought we lived in tipis and should be wearing moccasins. It was innocent enough, but that's a stereotype, and teachers need to realize that non-Indian children bring many stereotypes like that into the classroom. It is not enough for a teacher to think or worse, say, that "oh, that was just harmless. He didn't mean anything by it." A teacher's job is to educate. A teacher needs to think about how those "harmless" stereotypes affect Indian children, my children, in the classroom.

Please don't just teach about Indians in November (Thanksgiving)! And think about the stereotypes. Talking about buffalo makes less sense here, for example, since in the northwest the tradition is fishing not hunting buffalo on a horse. But if a teacher here talks about Indians like we all live in tepees and ride horses, well, teachers need to think about such stereotypes and their impact on *all* children. What is it that they really want children to learn about Indians?

Also, my family and I live on the Suquamish Reservation and the school sits right inside the boundaries of the Reservation. Yet, there is nothing about the Suquamish or even the Coast Salish up around the school. The art is by non-Native artists and its about Plains Indians! The school should reflect the Tribal Community whose children go there. On "Back-to-School" night, they serve Salmon "donated by the Tribe," but there is nothing there representing the tribe. Imagine if they invited the Elders of the Community or the Canoe Families to come and share songs and dances, or share some of their own experiences. Imagine if they did research to learn more about the Tribal Community. Imagine.

What Do You Want Teachers to Know About Your Children and Why?

Melody Bidtah

Some teachers don't seem to want our children to succeed or the teachers don't seem to be trying hard enough. For example, my nephew, he loves to weave. He weaves better than me, his aunt. He's a very good weaver. He loves his culture. He loves to sing traditional songs in the S'Klallam language.

He is a visual learner. Yet, his teacher faces him away from her in class. And all year my sister has fought to have him turned around, fought to have him taught in a way that going to have him be more successful. She has tried, but it has been very frustrating for her because he should be reading at a fourth grade level and he can only read at a second grade level. Where were the services that he needs to succeed? They weren't there. They weren't provided.

And, there is a side of the boy that the teacher probably doesn't see. He *loves* his cousins, he loves his younger brother and he loves his sister. He loves his family. He takes care of his little brother and watches out for him. He plays with my daughter, and treats her like a sister. He's very family-oriented and he teaches them things. He knows right from wrong and he will tell them so, if someone is doing something, he will let them know whether it is the right thing or not. If the teachers *knew that* about him *maybe* they would try differently to teach him in a way that he needs to be taught. Because he's not just a student who is failing, he is a *genuine caring boy* who's capable of doing anything. He can pull [paddle] a canoe and he can lead other children in a traditional dance. It's just the way he learns, and maybe some Indian children learn that way, they learn because it is part of their culture, learning by doing, learning by watching, *not* just by cutting paper and doing the same math problem fifty times.

Lovera Black Crow

Often Indian children are made fun of at school because they are "different" in the eyes of the non-Indian children. Indian children *are* different, but in another kind of way. Teachers may believe that every Indian child is different because of the color of his or her skin, or the shape of their eyes, or the length of their hair. However, the outward appearance isn't all that matters. The other kind of difference is that he or she has a thriving culture that lives within them.

Take for instance, my eldest daughter, Ralena. At the time, she was in second grade. There was an incident at her school where she was sent home with a "Rule Reminder" for the act she had done to another student in her class. I was to sign the Rule Reminder form and send it back with Ralena.

While I was upset with my daughter for what she had done, I was also concerned with *why* she had done this. She explained to me, with tears in her eyes, "Mom, she keeps calling me 'Chinese eyes' and 'Slanty' eyes and 'Poopy Color Eyes' girl." Of course, I was upset and angry. I asked if she had notified her (non-Native) teacher of what the (non-Native) little girl was saying to her and her response was, of course, "no."

Because Ralena had gotten in trouble, she was taking her punishment without any argument, as she had been raised. But because the non-Native girl had *not* gotten into trouble for calling her names, in Ralena's mind, the non-Native teacher was making it okay for *all* the non-Native children on the playground to make fun of her like this. Apparently, the non-Native girl had taunting my daughter for several weeks already about her skin tone, hair, and for being an "Injun"!

I explained that name-calling was not acceptable and that I would *not* tolerate this sort of racism against her, in her place of learning, where she is to feel safe and protected. I told my daughter to go to her teacher the next morning and tell her what her classmate had called her. She did so, but nothing happened.

So, seeing that nothing was going to happen to the little non-Native girl for what she had called my child, I went straight to the non-Native principal and the teacher. I followed all the proper procedures with my complaint as to why nothing had happened to this little non-Native girl for her acts of racism against my child. I wanted to know why the non-native child was not disciplined for her behavior as well. What she had done was just as bad as what my daughter had done to her, if not worse. In the end, I am still unsure if the non-Native child was sent home with a Rule Reminder about what she had done.

I realize that to the non-Native teacher it wasn't a big deal, it was just a simple Rule Reminder, but in my daughter's heart, she knows that from that day forward, it is *not* ok for another child to call her such names. She knows now, that her mother will not stand for it, ever! If I were to have let this incident go, my daughter would have gone on thinking it's ok for non-Native children to make fun of her because she appears different to them. now she knows, it is not okay. She knows that I care enough to take a stand for her.

Teachers need to know these *acts of racism do happen* to our children from elementary school up until their senior year in school. It is of utmost importance for non-Native teachers, principals and councilors to know this *does* happen to our Native children and although we can't stop it from happening, we *can* make sure it doesn't happen in their place of learning.

Kara Horton

My own children have various learning styles. My daughter can grasp the standard for institutional learning. She can read directions and understand things quickly. My sons learn differently. They are visual learners.

It is important to me that my children are not ignored, or pushed through the system. One of my sons' was flagged for Learning Disabilities Testing but he was *not* tested for three years after he was flagged. He has had a difficult time struggling with work and having teachers write comments like, "Just needs to apply himself and use class time more wisely," did not help his struggle with learning. He is now a junior and because of the last few years of "ignorance," he has basically given up on school. When a teacher constantly writes statements such as the above, they should be concerned for the student instead of placing blame on the student for not doing class work.

My children suffered the loss of their father at the beginning of the school year. While I do not ask special favors or exceptions for them, this should be taken into consideration in their education. They do grieve for their father and it takes time for this grief to pass. Their behavior is a direct result of this grief and I reiterate, I do not ask special favors, just *compassion* that they be allowed to grieve for their father.

Overall, had my children been treated as individuals from the start, instead of stereotyped, I believe their school years would have been more successful. I believe, had the school followed through, or had *just one* teacher taken the initiative to follow through with why one of my sons was "failing," his school career would have been more rewarding and he would not have the "I quit" attitude to this day.

Teaching, I know, is a tough job. Schools are over crowded. Still, Indian children have enough to deal with just from various traumas (like death), they do not need a teacher to tell them they "aren't smart" by placing them in a "special" class without testing. Teachers should be taught to identify why a student may not be their completing homework. Something may be going on at home and it can affect their learning. I don't expect teachers to be super teachers but there are basic common sense things a teacher ought to be able to identify and then work with our children toward a positive solution, rather than point fingers at students and label them as "unproductive."

Toni Jones

I think the most important thing for teachers who have Native children in their classroom is to not single them out, rather, allow them to express themselves in their own way. My younger daughter was in a music class and the non-Native teacher really embarrassed her because they started singing songs that they were making up about a cultural tradition here: the Bone Game. My daughter raised her hand to say that it wasn't right to make up songs about that because it was sacred. My daughter actually removed herself from the activity and refused to participate.

The songs about the Bone Game are culturally important and are not to be made fun of. Even though the word "game" is in the title, it was a serious game. The way we have been taught, it is not something that you mess around with. But the teacher used toothpicks for bones and embarrassed my daughter for not participating. She called my daughter the "Girl Who Didn't Participate" in the "Dances with Wolves" kind of way of naming, and the whole class made fun of her. My daughter was only ten. The teacher went on and mocked the seriousness of the game, my daughter, and our culture when she said, "Well, they *used* to play it." The teacher apparently didn't want to listen to my daughter, who understood the cultural meaning of the game, and knows it is still played today.

So, I think having the administrators and teachers involved in the Tribal Communities that they serve, would really help. Then they would get know and to see that the Tribal Communities are different, rather than reading it from some book, which might not even be accurate. And then, maybe teachers wouldn't make fun of our cultures in the classroom, at our children's expense!

CONCLUSION

We, as American Indian women and mothers, don't ask for favoritism or special treatment. We *do* ask that our children be respected. We *do* ask that our children's needs and cultural differences be honored. We *do* ask that our children and our cultures not be targets of mockery and ridicule by teachers or other students. We *do* ask that teachers get to know our Tribal Communities and learn who we are, not by books alone, but by coming to our events and meeting us and seeing our children outside of the predominantly white context. Maybe in these ways, bridges may be made so that our children will experience greater success in public schools.

NOTE

1. I use the terms "American Indian," "Native Peoples," "Native" and "Native American" interchangeably. I purposefully capitalize "Native Nation" and "Nation" to respect the tribal sovereignty of the tribes.

CHAPTER TEN

The Role of Teacher Beliefs in the Bilingual/Bicultural Classroom

MARION LYNCH

I have been working as a supervising professor during student teaching practice with the teacher candidates participating in this project (over the course of one year). The teacher candidates are immigrants or children of immigrants from the Dominican Republic, Trinidad, Tobago, Yemen and Jamaica. There is a rich diversity within these countries—east Indian, Spanish, Caribbean, Arab, African descent, and Chinese. One teacher stated: ". .in my country the great challenge in teaching was the competition between 'local dialects' and 'standard English' which were both variations of the English language." The participants have all had firsthand experience in a bicultural and/or bilingual setting. For our teaching candidates, it has been a long journey to appreciate their own bicultural/bilingual heritage in society which has not always been responsive to their heritage or culture. . Nevertheless, at this point in their lives, they know that in a global economy there are definite advantages being bilingual and bicultural, which makes it easier for them to focus on the needs of children in multicultural classes.

I have heard many times throughout my pedagogical endeavors that a teacher's cultural background plays an important role in the classroom. In one of my graduate classes my professor stated that "students learn best from teachers with the same cultural background. Never having identified with my own cultural background (Irish/English), I remember feeling quite uneasy about this. Being Irish and English is something I was taught to say, but did not feel it was a description of who I was. I never really knew much about my cultural background until I became a teacher and read a book to my class, about the Irish potato famine, *Nory Ryan's Song.* This book, this story, was the first time that I identified with my cultural background—I connected with the stories and have memorized all of the good and bad luck superstitions my family passed on to me. The day I witnessed one of my students "knocking on wood" I discovered that I passed a little of my "culture" down to my "family of students." This is the day I realized my college professor may have been wrong: our school family has lots of different cultures and traditions that we share, and it is this sharing and openness to differences that binds us together. Perhaps culture does play an important role in the class, it is an opportunity to teach respecting cultural differences, and the love that holds us together despite those differences.

This piece represents collective experiences our teachers have related regarding employing their cultural beliefs in the classroom in order to make instruction more meaningful for bicultural students. These narratives document frustrations with schools of education that do not provide adequate preparation and school systems that lack adequate resources to meet the needs of all students.

PERSONAL BELIEFS AND VALUES

In order to determine what personal beliefs and values impact their instruction, the teacher candidates created a list of their cultural beliefs and values that are reflected in instruction. They responded to statements such as:

" I believe in _____ because _____ ."

Although there were differences among them, there were common elements as well as a belief in a higher power. In addition the participants indicated that one's cultural background should be valued in the classroom; accomplishments come from strong family ties and conviction to succeed; all students deserve a proper education, teachers should prepare students for life experiences as well as academic achievement; a good education is key to succeed in America; and those entering the profession should have a passion and innate love for teaching and learning.

One value that was emphasized was the importance of a good education being reinforced via family experiences. Although some experienced cultural diversity in their home country, they agreed teaching in the United States is more challenging because students are who are bilingual/bicultural are coming from countries that span the globe. In a bicultural class teachers meet English language learners with varying degrees of facility with English. What may seem to be a daunting task has not diminished their determination. As future teachers, they consider it their responsibility to teach and assist students so that they will achieve and succeed.

UNDERGRADUATE TEACHER EDUCATION PROGRAMS

The teacher candidates were quick to point out aspects of their undergraduate education that had been particularly important in teaching. For example, they highlighted educators whose ideas have influenced their thinking and teaching such as John Dewey, Paulo Freire and Howard Gardner. In many ways, these "giant" educator experts have reinforced their personal beliefs and values. However, they did not believe their undergraduate education programs adequately prepared them for bicultural classrooms which are increasingly the norm in today's public schools. They stated that the main contradiction had been the unrealistic portrayal of schools. For example, they believed that more classes should be offered in the undergraduate teacher education programs that focused on issues in a bicultural classroom since they were confronted with these challenges on a daily basis.

The questions undergraduate programs can address but are not limited to are: How should teachers address student needs in a bicultural classroom? How can we maximize the use of limited resources to teach in meaningful ways? How should teachers respond with the ongoing pervasive high stakes testing, which ultimately detracts from teaching in depth and continues to satisfy the neoliberal political agenda rather than meaningful educational goals. In addition, pre-service teacher education programs should also include the analysis and evaluation of resources and materials for suitability with bicultural/bilingual populations. These future teachers believe that the greatest challenge facing new teachers is to find a balance between theory and practice capable of enhancing instruction in the bicultural/bilingual classroom. Finally, issues about the bicultural/bilingual classroom should be an integral/significant part of undergraduate teacher education experience with time devoted to alternative teaching models and how to best meet the needs of learners.

CULTURALLY RELEVANT PEDAGOGY

In many inner city schools (New York, Chicago, Los Angeles, etc.), students who were once considered to be in the minority now constitute the majority, with classrooms reflecting a bicultural mosaic. The pedagogy teachers are implementing reflects a greater focus on meeting the needs of bicultural students. Comprehensive changes are often made to the curriculum to accommodate this new reality. Appropriate materials are chosen by teachers that promote the bicultural students' learning. For example, resources and classroom materials are sensitive to students and reflect their cultural background, providing a necessary bridge from home language/culture to United Statian English and United Statian culture. A more challenging task is to synthesize and adapt publishers' materials that are often not suitable for a particular school population. While teachers from the same cultural background might find it easier to attempt these tasks, they also believe that all teachers should be able to make the necessary changes in a curriculum, that is, teachers in bicultural classes should be trained to maximize and adapt materials whether or not they share similar cultural backgrounds with students.

FUTURE TEACHERS' FAMILY LIFE EXPERIENCES

The cultural influences and their own family values encourage the teaching candidates to hold students accountable and to develop a sense of responsibility for their learning. They are well aware of the need to nurture students both emotionally and academically. This means that students are encouraged to speak openly about situations, express their feelings and have an ongoing dialogue with the teacher. When students can speak freely, they become self-motivated, gain a strong sense of self, and can rise above any situation. Their life experiences have taught them that it is necessary to use a variety of methods to enhance self-esteem, for example, group instruction, one-on-one conferencing, acknowledging student efforts.

An area that all our teaching candidates agreed upon is that the involvement of the parents while teachers maintain an open communication with families leads to greater student success. Therefore, learning about the background of students and keeping parents informed is an essential construct of their own pedagogy. Our teachers are also sensitive to the economic and social vicissitudes students may experience in families and single parent households. In many instances, daily existence is more about survival than education. These teachers constantly encourage students to do well and invite parents to play a greater role in helping raise the expectations of students. Relying on family experiences within the curriculum is key to optimizing learning in a bicultural classroom. Life experiences can be incorporated to begin the learning process and are helpful for students to start their journey of writing about unfamiliar topics. Classroom students can "turn and talk" about their home experiences. They can be drawn into the discussion as they relate their own life experience as a point of reference. Similarly, with a writing assignment, the teacher can model writing stories about her/his own life as a bicultural person. . Students can comprehend that their teacher has similar experiences and may encourage their own explorations.

Word play can engage bicultural students in joint thinking that benefit English language acquisition. The students challenge themselves to think about as many synonyms a word may have, even if the synonym is in another language. When these words are incorporated in discussions, students feel proud of their heritage and are able to participate in classroom discussions rather than sitting quietly with nothing to offer. When teachers are not familiar with home languages, which is more often the case, then the teacher must trust students' word knowledge and engage other students who may be able to assist in the meaning of a new word. The ultimate goal is that students realize that being bicultural is not negative but is very positive in helping them academically as well as in life experiences.

TEACHERS' ROLE

The role of our teachers takes on new meaning when in addition to academic support and implementation of standards there is additional nurturing, guidance, and mentoring all leading to academic success. In order to do this, many argue that one must be comfortable with one's own cultural background and heritage. Some teacher candidates explained that it took many years before they began to feel confident and good about their backgrounds and themselves. Thus, they recognize that feeling confident and attaining a good education is the first step to succeed and pursue one's dreams. They experienced clarity from mentors with similar backgrounds who encouraged them and provided guidance and information, which enabled them to move forward in their education. One participant cites how a Latina professor sought her out and counseled her to consider bilingual education and apply for a fellowship. This professor encouraged her to apply for a fellowship to continue her studies. Thus, she was able to complete her studies with a Master's degree in Bilingual Education. She stated:

> "now students turn to me for guidance in the same way I turned to others who helped me accept my bicultural heritage. I am not only my students' teacher, I am a role model and mentor."

For these teacher candidates, mentoring is an important part of their role as teachers—they do not believe that there are enough positive role models in society to help students move beyond their present world and begin to broaden their vision and expand their life experiences into other areas of learning. Therefore, their commitment as mentors is paramount and they transmit this to students by helping them build self-esteem, set high academic standards, and feel good about their heritage.

We recognize that every child comes to school with different needs and experiences to share in a bicultural class. Our teachers set standards not only to prepare students for academic success but for life experiences as well. Preparation for culturally diverse students is not just about academic achievement; it should also include success for life after school. The teacher's work is more than just teaching the curriculum; it is also about non-academic moments to engage in "heart-to-heart" talks that can lead to confidence and trust. In this way, our teachers bridge the gap between students' home culture existence and that which is new. Thus, encouraging students and helping them develop self-confidence is an important role in the instructional process.

DIFFERENTIATED INSTRUCTION (ALONG WITH CULTURALLY RELEVANT PEDAGOGY)

Differentiated instruction (along with culturally relevant pedagogy) is at the heart of teaching in a bicultural/bilingual classroom—it takes time, reflection, and constant change. Our teachers know how to organize instruction for differentiated learning so that all students learn. Differentiated instruction gives the teacher opportunities to really get to know students, work with them individually, and use creative approaches to address their needs. Differentiated instruction enables teachers to exercise a great deal of autonomy, as they design meaningful lessons to address the needs of students during small group instruction or with an individual student. However, a word of caution: lessons should have substance and not be reduced to "decorative" notations. For example, if a lesson is about germination, then the focus should not be turned from science into an art lesson where students are drawing seeds or making sunflowers. The lesson may be great for art, but may not meet science objectives to teach germination. Therefore, the lesson should be focused and information offered in multiple modes so that students are given opportunities to learn from different perspectives and present information in multiple modes as well.

In addition, our teachers constantly search for new ways to present creative and interesting lessons to capture the attention of their students. For example, with older students, real life experiences capture a students attention and ultimately affect their lives, for example, during student government campaigns, students become involved in all aspects of a campaign, promotion, voter registration, mock conventions, and casting ballots. Another example is to engage students in the same way to contribute information about their cultural backgrounds and experiences. Students bring items from home to facilitate class discussions and provide opportunities to contribute to the lesson using meaningful life experiences. When bicultural students are given opportunities to engage in participatory activities it is a very effective learning process.

STANDARDIZED TESTING AND SCRIPTED LESSONS

Curriculum that is pre-packaged has little benefit for teachers or students. The needs of students in a bicultural classroom cannot be met with a "one size fits all" curriculum. A lot of time and money is invested in performance testing and assessment but little time is spent on how best to teach them. How will they succeed if they only study subjects superficially without having comprehensive discussions and opportunities to be great thinkers? Students need time and practice learning to think for themselves and question ideas. How can they do this if we are only interested in training them to pass timed tests? We need to mold our future generation of doctors, lawyers, teachers, and other professionals to be thinkers. Teachers are bombarded with testing standards, with strict policies from school administrators, who are in turn also forced to succumb to pressures from others. They understand the need for assessment; it is valuable and necessary. But testing should serve the purpose of enhancing instruction, changing direction, or setting a new course. It is when it becomes excessive and overwhelming for students and teachers that the purpose is lost. This overemphasis on testing leaves teachers frustrated as it takes away precious instruction time and little opportunity to utilize data. What we are seeing is that teachers are burned out and disillusioned.

Although today's educational standards have evolved to reflect more student autonomy and lessons that incorporate topics to address today's world, the constraints contradict these efforts. Instead, our educational system uses a "cookie cutter" approach to mold students into placidity and conformity. This makes it difficult to really address the needs of diverse populations. Having policy which demands that all students be on the same page on the same day does not acknowledge the concept of differentiated instruction (nor culturally relevant pedagogy)

Finally, for these teachers, self-reflection is an important check on their instructional methods. It enables us to change our approach to meet students' needs, to make certain that students' voices are heard and that students know that their voices matter. This is the time to evaluate the instruments we use to assess students' work, to assess whether materials were appropriate. This is also the time to determine which methods and strategies are effective and what needs to be changed to reach all students. All students deserve a good education in preparation for life and dreams.

CHAPTER ELEVEN

Responsive Teaching

Our Muslim Students' Learning Expectations

LENA BOUSTANI DARWICH

A student told me her story a few semesters ago. Since then, I begin every unit and every teacher in-service and teacher training on students' religious diversity with this same story. I am certain you have heard a story just like it in one context or another, and it has moved you. It has moved you to think about how your classroom culture may clash with your students' religion, and it has moved you to reflect on your views of your students and on your classroom practices. This is Ayisha's story:

> The teacher is not taking us seriously. I've explained to her when she asked me once during Parent Orientation and again during Parent/Teacher conferences, and I wrote her a note that we are Muslim and don't celebrate Christian holidays or Halloween or Thanksgiving or Valentine. It is not our belief. She suggested that if she were doing any activities that particularly focus on holidays like these, that she would give my daughter another worksheet to do. I thanked her for her understanding and willingness to work with my daughter. But my daughter has had to go to her teacher and ask her for these worksheets. That doesn't bother her as much as what her teacher always says to her: "Only if that is what you really want, dear!" Perhaps it is the teacher's way of encouraging freedom of choice, but my daughter is eight. She feels confused and doesn't want to go to school on some days. I am distressed for my daughter. I think her teacher will be doing the Easter egg hunt next week. How do I help my daughter not feel uneasy about going to school that day or about asking for another worksheet? It just seems that the teacher is undermining me, undermining our beliefs—why?

I couldn't think of a textbook answer to Ayisha's question. She wanted and deserved an affirmation of her and her daughter's right to their beliefs. The one thing I thought I could do was hold classroom discussions on this issue. And one day, a colleague suggested I write an essay for a book on bicultural and bilingual students. It was the best suggestion. So I began to write this chapter hoping to open a window through which we can look into some of our Muslim students' experiences in classrooms where their religious identity is ignored or, worse yet, attacked. It is my hope that what we see will help us begin thinking about and implementing instructional accommodations that can make our classrooms inviting and safe environments for our Muslim students. The thoughts and reflections in this chapter are based on qualitative observations I made as a classroom teacher, a university instructor, and a Muslim. I will not be presenting thick descriptions of the Muslim students from whom I learned so much; but instead I have interlaced some of their stories to highlight issues they themselves identify as central for their success in our public schools. A teacher once pulled me to the side at an in-service and told me that she did not want to seem patronizing especially after my talk, but she loved all her students the same and wanted the same for all of them, even after she met them and learned they were white or Chinese or Muslim. "After all," she added, "weren't we all created equal?" Again, I couldn't think of a textbook answer! I stood looking at her silently questioning my commitment to differentiated instruction. The Eureka moment didn't happen for me until a few days later. Yes, it is true that Muslim students are in many ways similar to all other students. They attend our public schools, engage in learning activities, participate in social functions, and compete in athletic events. Many are bilingual and/or bicultural. The important difference is in their religion. Is this difference significant enough to merit our attention? It is. Why? Because religion is an aspect of identity that is present in our students' conversations about themselves, and, not surprisingly, our Muslim students identify themselves in terms relating them to their religion Islam.

It is impractical to say that our Muslim students are like all or any other students. It is also impractical to generalize. They represent numerous racial, ethnic and linguistic groups. They are the children of indigenous Muslims, mostly African Americans, converts, and immigrants who come from all over the globe. The Muslim population is estimated at 1.25 billion worldwide. About one-fifth of Muslims are from the Arab World, North Africa, Turkey, Iran, and Afghanistan; almost one-third of Muslims are from the Indian subcontinent and Pakistan; one-third are from Southeast Asia, Indonesia, and Central and Sub-Saharan Africa; and about one-fifth are from Europe, China, Australia, and the Americas. Muslim students also represent many socio-economic groups. They are the children of factory workers, doctors, teachers, farmers, bankers, single parents, etc.

However, there are specific religious factors common to most Muslim students that shape their responses to instruction. As teachers, we can enhance their achievement by responding to these factors. Our best recourse is to learn about our students, their experiences, and their expectations.

KNOWLEDGE IS THE GATEWAY TO SUCCESS

Hanaa is soft-spoken and has an engaging personality. She is excited about her advanced placement test scores and talks about the upper level courses she will take at college. She is eager to learn as much as she can. I ask her why.

"I learn because I know how much knowledge is important." (Hanaa, 12th grade).

A central factor that shapes Muslim students' response to instruction is the belief that knowledge and the acquisition of knowledge are valuable. Islamically, knowledge of the religion of Islam, knowledge of the basic Islamic beliefs and the Islamic rules, is held in highest regard. Muslims believe that they earn rewards by having knowledge of and implementing the rules of the religion. They sincerely strive to learn about their religion, and they pass this belief on to their children. It is very consistent for Muslim students to transfer these ethics to their classroom experiences and strive to learn classroom content. In this way they are intrinsically motivated to succeed. Adam and Sally illustrate this when they talk about their role as students and what they think is the role of their teachers:

"I think my teacher's job is to help me understand and break down the materials. My job is to pay attention, do the work, and think about matching my answers to her questions." (Adam, 12th grade)

Adam is saying that teachers who wish to see their Muslim students succeed scaffold them. They use a variety of instructional strategies and learning activities that complement their students' enthusiasm for learning. They challenge their students and allow them to work through meaningful problems. They use various strategies and activities to provide students with opportunities to fully explore content and construct their own learning. Sally adds that teachers must take care to provide purpose and relevance for these activities:

"Teachers should make sure students understand the material and can apply it to what they want to do later on, to real life situations." (Sally, 12th grade)

Perhaps the first step in responding to Sally's comment is to recognize who is voicing it. It could be any one of our students, but it comes now from Sally—who is a Muslim student.

The responsive teacher connects with this specific piece of information on identity and institutes effective instructional devices. These devices will help Sally find meaning and purpose in what she learns and help prepare her for her future. Many instructional strategies that allow students to organize and represent knowledge in their own way are extremely effective because they engage students and require them to express their learning as individuals. However, more is needed when we want to provide Sally with courage to realize opportunities and take on challenges otherwise denied to her and others like her, by those smug in persistent refutation of diversity. We need to encourage our students' sense of pride in self so that they can own their future. Heightening our students' awareness of their heritage is the most effective way I have found to impress upon them that their expectations are truly theirs, that their learning is truly theirs, and that their future is truly theirs. In the case of our Muslim students, we should include discussions about the sweeping achievements in mathematics and physical sciences Muslim scholars have achieved as well as their impressive history of leadership in medicine, to name a few examples.

INSTRUCTIONAL STRATEGIES AND LEARNING ACTIVITIES

A second factor that shapes Muslim students' response to instruction is the respect for the learned scholars of Islam that is encouraged by the religion. Learned scholars are awarded the ranks of honor and deference. They are considered the teachers, the Imams. Muslims seek these scholars' counsel on religious and secular issues. Muslim parents instill this respect for the learned scholars in their children and teach them to ask questions and require corroboration. Again, it is consistent for Muslim students to respect learning in their classroom teachers. Of additional significance is that many Muslim students, particularly of middle school and high school age, take conscious steps in determining the level of respect to give each of their teachers. Factors in this decision making process include not only the relevance of the instructional content but their personal view of the teacher's motivation and goals for teaching. They expect their teachers to have the students' interest and success at heart, because they, as Muslims, are taught to be considerate and desire goodwill for others. Omar's favorite teacher is his soccer coach. He says it's because his coach talks about good and bad plays and about each player's strengths and weaknesses. He helps them with skills and explains plays to them.

> "He knows what he's talking about. He played college soccer and knows what we go through and what it means to win! He wants us to know that feeling too." (Omar, 10th grade)

I think what Omar is also saying is that teachers who wish to encourage a strong academic relationship between themselves and their Muslim students must be student-centered. They must also demonstrate content mastery and deliver subject matter in a confident manner. They must provide the rationale for learning a concept or mastering a task. They must include various sources of information, present various perspectives, relate arguments, and provide alternative solutions. And, they must welcome questions from their students and admit not having all the answers.

> "I listen to my teacher when he can answer my questions. I am very good at Math; I want my teacher to teach me Math! I don't want to just get through the book." (Ahmed, 7th grade)

Ahmed is telling us what he wants. Many teacher/student relationships break down because we don't know what our student wants. We have our ideas of what he or she needs, but this is not enough to build relationships. Teachers must listen to their students because it is not easy for students to be diverse and outspoken. For many, it takes most of their effort to affirm their identity in classrooms, hallways, and cafeterias where no one else looks like them. They have no energy or inclination to ask for or demand anything else.

Teachers need to be consistent in their practices. Many students are aware of the level of their teachers' dedication to their learning, and they base their conclusions about the effectiveness of these teachers on this awareness. Those of us who impress our students with our knowledge and our consistency earn their time and attention. The others lose the opportunity to connect with their students. Yasmeen is nine years old. Logical ordering of events is key to understanding her experiences. Consistency is logical to her; anything else confuses her.

> "I raised my hand. It's one of the rules to raise our hands before we answer a question. She wouldn't call on me." (Yasmeen, 3rd grade)

I expect that Yasmeen stopped raising her hand before she spoke and probably ignored several other classroom rules.

COOPERATION AND ACCOUNTABILITY

A third factor that shapes Muslim students' response to instruction is the sense of cooperation and the building of community encouraged by Islamic teachings. Muslims are encouraged to visit each other, to come to each other's aid, to partake of meals as in the breaking of their fast during the month of Ramadan, and to pray together. These practices develop and strengthen cooperative skills necessary to building a community. Muslim students participate in these practices and bring their understanding of the concept of cooperation and their skills at participating in group work to their classrooms. Teachers can strengthen these skills by allowing for various cooperative learning and reciprocal teaching activities. They can enhance these activities for their Muslim students by assigning them leadership roles and by explicitly defining the criteria to be achieved.

Muslim students understand the concept of accountability and realize the importance of staying on task. Islamic teachings stress that adults are responsible for the choices they make and accountable for the results of their choices. Teachers who wish to foster this sense of accountability provide clear guidelines, taking care that they encourage independent thinking. They monitor their students' progress and provide constructive feedback. They allow their students to search for and discover their own answers and own learning. Amer and Tareq express this very well in their own words:

> "[The teacher's name] Ms. Martin is my favorite teacher…I know exactly what she wants, and I can tell when I've done what she wants us to do, we all can! She lets us know it." (Amer, 8th grade)

Amer is in a comfort zone because his teacher has made her expectations and her goals clear for him. He does not have to guess at what he has to do. This frees him to work wholly on his task. Tareq understands the importance of clear expectations too. He also seems to grasp the importance of scaffolding. He says that:

> "Sometimes I am not sure if I am thinking of the right steps to solve a problem. It helps me when my teacher asks questions that make me think…that make me remember…not just tell me the answer." (Tareq, 11th grade)

WAIT TIME

A fourth factor that shapes Muslim students' response to instruction deals with the Islamic teachings that emphasize the importance of monitoring one's words. Muslims are taught the importance of words and the need to be prudent with their use. Islamically appropriate words earn one rewards; inappropriate words may lead to disrepute and even blasphemy. For example, reciting the Qur'an earns one great rewards; ridiculing a fellow Muslim subtracts from one's rewards. Muslims teach their children to be cautious in their responses. Again, it is consistent that Muslim children conduct their classroom interactions with self-monitoring and self-editing. Teachers who understand this concept realize that their Muslim students' concerns go beyond the practical use of language and allow the student several seconds of wait time to respond to their questions and to the class discussions. They do not insist on immediate answers and do not show or imply impatience with the student. Alyia is frustrated when her teachers or her classmates answer for her. She wants to be given the extra seconds to phrase her responses as best she can.

> "I know the answer, I just want to take my time to think about phrasing it in the best way I can." (Alyia, 10th grade)

Hasan explains that he does not need any remedial help. He wants to be allowed to participate on his own terms. He wants to be allowed to think. This is what he has to say:

> "It isn't that I am slow. Sometimes I know the answer before my teacher finishes asking the question…I know what I mean, but I can't just blurt it out. I used to participate a lot, but not so much now…someone blurts something out, or the teacher just doesn't give me a chance. I don't want to say the wrong words." (Hasan, 11th grade)

APPEARANCES AND IDENTITY

Rana and Darine are best friends. They are inseparable. Both wear the newest fashions, but somehow Rana is the one who gets the more obvious stares.

> "They [some teachers and students] look at me. I am not sure whether they see me, or they're thinking that I'm backwards." (Rana, 9th grade)

You see, Rana wears the Hijab, or the Islamic head and body covering for women. Darine doesn't, but she is always modestly dressed. Darine supports her friend. Sometimes she stares back, but lately she talks too. She explains that wearing of the Hijab is not "some throwback to an age of women enslavement," but it represents a woman's statement of commitment to her beliefs.

Darine and Rana's story illustrates a major factor that influences Muslim students' response to the learning interaction: the modesty in dress for men and women required by Islam. Many female Muslim students wear the Hijab. Their dress choices indicate their adherence to the requirement of modesty and reaffirm their Muslim identity. Several of the Muslim students I spoke with claimed that the initial responses to their appearance caused them concern. They felt that their teachers and peers perceived them as "strange." These students felt isolated and were hesitant to participate in class activities or to socialize with their classmates. They questioned the need to remain in classrooms where they were not appreciated for who they were or given the chance to express themselves. Crystal is willing to talk but only when she feels there is genuine interest in what she has to say:

> "I don't want my teacher to ask me if I don't get hot wearing long sleeves or where do I buy my scarves. I want my teacher to want to know about me, what I believe, how I live. When I feel that she really wants to know, I will approach her." (Crystal, 11th grade)

Many Muslim students have positive feelings about classroom dynamics. They trust the sensibility of their classmates and teachers because they feel that their teachers and friends can look beyond appearances.

> "Usually, their first thought is not so positive. But, after they get to know me, many say that Muslims have a lot of integrity, and they like the fact that they know me. They stop trying to enforce opinions they heard about Muslims on me." (Nadjia, 11th grade)

Nadjia is saying that we need to reflect about our views and opinions. Relationships between teachers and students and students and students are jeopardized when we assume things due to lack of knowledge or lack of understanding. Teachers who wish to include their Muslim students in the learning interaction begin by reflecting upon their own perceptions and beliefs about Islam and Muslims. They acknowledge any stereotypes and prejudice as negative factors and consider the identity of their Muslim students in a positive manner. They learn about their students and become involved in their daily lives and tasks by asking genuine questions, questions for the sake of true understanding and not simply to be polite. They correct erroneous information in the classroom and help all students understand that their Muslim peers are not personally responsible for negative events depicted in the media. They are tolerant and, most importantly, teach tolerance to all their students. And, they are ready to invoke their school policy against possible harassment of their Muslim students. Noah expresses this in a most powerful statement:

> "He [Noah's teacher] treated me in a different way. But after some time, he learned and treated me appropriately. He stopped trying to make me believe that what he knew was fact. He started to see that Muslims do not see everything the way he does...that they aren't, what he thought." (Noah, 11th grade)

All of the Muslim students I spoke with felt a responsibility to talk about Islam to their teachers and classmates. They felt strongly that many at their schools were unaware of basic information regarding Islam and the beliefs of Muslims or had the wrong impressions. They wanted to share their knowledge and experiences with their teachers and classmates. As teachers, we need to capitalize on their willingness to do so because, if we want to enhance our students' learning and broaden their world-views, we must encourage the exchange of knowledge.

> "It makes me sad that my friends don't know...they should know. I would tell them." (Rayhanna, 6th grade)

I would listen to Rayhanna and to all my students, because as I learn more about them, I help them discover more about themselves. In this, I help my students affirm their identity and participate with more confidence. No student will feel alienated.

"Some of my teachers ask me about the different Muslim Holidays, about fasting in Ramadan…about Muslim values…I see how many of my values help me be a better student. I also see that I don't need to hide or tone down who I am just so that I fit in." (Suzanne, 12th grade)

CONCLUSION

Most of the Muslim students I spoke with made reference to the fact that they work hard, are "smart," and achieve their goals. Many admitted that they put much effort into completing their work and enjoy what their efforts bring them. For example, Nabil (10th grade) earns the highest scores in his college preparatory Calculus class. Omar (8th grade) wins praise from his teachers and classmates for his riveting short stories. Abed (12th grade) is captain of his school's varsity basketball team. Teachers who wish to enhance the academic achievement of their Muslim students do not just look beyond appearances but maintain high expectations and inspire confidence. They provide mastery goals and various challenging activities, which include collaborative learning activities. They hold their students strictly accountable for their work. They encourage an enduring positive sense of self, support intrinsic motivation, and applaud their students' successes.

"A teacher might feel that having a Muslim student is a burden, but on the contrary, it is a good thing." (Dana, 12th grade)

CHAPTER TWELVE

Exploration for School Action-Based Learning

NOELLE GENTILE

In our democratic society, individuals are slowly losing their voice. Our environment is endangered, violence surrounds us, mega-corporations shape policy and politics, racial tensions are ever-present, and we are a nation at war internally and abroad. In light of the complex challenges we face as a modern society, it is imperative for students to learn at an early age to not only be socially conscious, but to be problem solvers and agents of change. My journey as an elementary school teacher in one of the nation's most diverse cities has taught me how critical it is to raise our individual and collective voices and identify and respond to problems through action. In the following story, I will document a two-year process which resulted in the creation of curriculum infused with action-based learning. It was the explorations of social issues within a diverse community setting that inspired the curriculum.

Last year, my third grade class spent time analyzing and exploring the implications of the words of Mahatma Gandhi, "Be the change you want to see in the world." It is by providing students with the opportunity to share prior knowledge of their own culture and experiences within a community setting that they can begin to process their environment, and embrace the opportunity to be the change they envision in the world around them. By participating in social justice units, students became problem solvers capable of tackling the social injustices that occur in their own classroom, neighborhood, and the world. Often educators underestimate students' deep and valuable perceptions of the world around them.

While it is important for classrooms to be safe havens for children, it is no less important to ensure that their education feels relevant to their lives, especially for bilingual, biracial, and bicultural children. By creating a curriculum that both infuses social justice and encourages student exchange within a safe community setting, the level of respect and engagement in the classroom will rise.

The learning that takes place within the classroom will tap into students' prior knowledge. As a result, students will have ownership over their education. When teachers connect curriculum to topics that are relevant to the everyday lives of students, students' engagement with learning will increase. For example, this year, projects included: teaching history through the lens of a particular cultural identity, drawing on the "expert" insights of students of that particular bilingual/bicultural group; raising awareness for contemporary social issues through fund-raising projects (i.e., hurricane relief aid, global warming); and implementing a student conflict resolution counselor program. By these means, students' engagement with and ownership over their own learning process are expected to increase. This excitement will in turn engage students in other areas of academics and eliminate many management issues. In order for our students to be the agents of change they wanted to see in the world, we first needed to form a strong community within the classroom. Outlined in what follows are steps we took to form a community in order to collectively take action and ultimately take action in the world around us.

WHO

Twenty-four students constituted an inclusion classroom at P.S.8 Robert Fulton School located in Brooklyn Heights. While Brooklyn Heights is an affluent neighborhood, the school serves a diverse socio-economic population, with many students residing outside of Brooklyn Heights. The school has been in transition (grants have brought economic change and enrichment programs, an influx of new teachers and administration) for the last several years. Socio-economic statuses of parents affect resources available to children in schools. A school's location is paramount in determining how a community can assist in making the changes necessary to ensure respectable test scores. Its doors were on the verge of closing forever due to low attendance and test scores when a group of neighborhood parents came together in order to make school-wide improvement. During the 2006-2007 school years, my classroom included students, one African student, three biracial students (two African American and Euro-American students and one African and French student), five White students, two Latino students, and one Indian student. Ten of the 24 students were special education students with Individual Education Plans (IEP:

a detailed program which outlines tailored goals and expectations in order to meet individual students' needs). This made my classroom bilingual, biracial, and bicultural, but also diverse in the fact that there were IEP children.

This classroom was rich with cultural, economic, and academic diversity. The academic and emotional diversity that is inherent in an inclusion classroom can be demanding, but if the diversity in all areas is acknowledged, and appreciated, rather than merely tolerated, it can contribute to learning in all areas. I worked alongside Jonathan Garber (a special education teacher) with these students for two years, looping them from second 2nd to third 3rd grade.

FORMING A COMMUNITY

We knew that in order to teach students to be imaginative problem solvers, equipped with the tools to examine and be agents for social change, it was critical to form a safe and supportive community setting in the classroom. This community would be one that would, to foster free exchange of ideas, encourage risk-taking as well as introduce and examine a diversity of perspectives. In 2005-2006, Mr. Garber and I worked to create an environment which fostered constant dialogue about the world in which we live, individual cultural identities, and a collective classroom identity. There was an open invitation for questions and concerns, where students knew they could use the community meetings to process not only their academic world but the outside world as well. Students would frequently bring in newspaper articles of stories that upset, confused, or excited them. Students were encouraged to answer one another's questions by prompting them with, "What do you think?" Families were also encouraged to keep us abreast with any changes or issues in the students' lives. By instructing curriculum through the lens of the struggles and concerns students dealt with outside of school, we were better able to engage students in classroom work as well as meet individual needs more effectively.

Both students and families began to utilize the community as a place to truly understand themselves and others. Kyle, a biracial student with a fair complexion, was having difficulty processing the duality of his cultural make-up. Due to his appearance, Kyle was not able to identify with his African American culture. His mother, who is of African American descent, was concerned and brought this issue to our attention. We responded with a read-aloud of a book, which describes a child's journey to understanding and appreciates his bicultural background.

This activity served as an entry point for conversations that focused on the beauty of having a bicultural and biracial background. Another student named John, who is bilingual and biracial, whose parents are of African and French descent, struggled with similar issues and through this process developed a friendship with Kyle via open dialogue. This forum allowed both boys to gain confidence in themselves and become proud of their backgrounds. Eventually students began to deem it as "cool" to be biracial. As a result of these honest and open conversations, our students began to see our community as a safe place to share issues in their lives.

THE UNPLANNED LESSON

Too often we are encouraged to protect children from the "real world" and issues that they will inevitably face as they continue to grow up. Many parents and educators consider these issues to be either too upsetting or simply above the grasp of students' understanding. Instead, we are encouraged to teach a sterile social studies unit informing rote facts about several countries. But when we study countries and different cultures within the context of facts and statistics, are we actually providing children a sense of world communities? Are we transporting them? Are we acknowledging the vast cultures they represent?

> Perhaps travel cannot prevent bigotry, but by demonstrating that all peoples cry, laugh,eat, worry, and die, it can introduce the idea that if we try and understand each other, we may even become friends (from *Title* by Maya Angelou)

It is the teacher's job to transport the students into other places by giving them rich experiences within the classroom. We utilized both the community and students' diversity in order to address social justice in the classroom.

A social issues unit that instructs history while addressing the community within the classroom and the larger world outside of the classroom can be taught in many ways. One way is a formal curriculum unit created and explored by the students and teachers throughout the year. Other times it is less formal, such as a teacher capitalizing on a teachable moment.

A small group of eight- and nine-year-olds gathered around to listen to a read-aloud about the origins of The Great Wall of China. Before I began, I reminded my students that one of their classmates, Peter, was Chinese and had spent many summers in China (he is a first generation Chinese American), and that he may be able to provide additional information. Peter was a particularly shy student, who gained confidence by identifying with and sharing his personal experience of his numerous visits to his homeland.

At times students of different racial and bicultural backgrounds are seen as experts on their particular racial and cultural group. This alleged expertise some teachers place upon bilingual/bicultural students could put additional pressure upon students to speak for a whole racial and cultural group. In this instance, Peter is a student who I know takes great pride in sharing stories of his culture; he was more than happy to speak and his face lit with glee. Soon after, I realized Ed, a Puerto Rican student, held his hands over his ears. When I asked Ed what was wrong, he responded by saying, "I don't like talking about people being different. I don't like saying that Peter is Chinese." His answer gave me insight into one of my student's perception of race. Over the course of the year we had several open discussions about race in order to address the vast racial make-up of the community. It became clear to me that while we had many open discussions about race and culture over the year, for Ed there was a disconnect between describing someone's race in a way that accepts or investigates their culture and not discussing someone's culture (because by doing so we acknowledge a difference). Ed realized that by acknowledging Peter's ethnicity, we were acknowledging that Peter was different. Ed went on to state that it was not a good thing to say that someone was different. "We are all the same!" he stated.

We live in a society that has been trained to view the acknowledgment of racial difference as a negative occurrence; as a result, many people of color are made to feel invisible or stripped of their racial identity. At this point, I knew I had to address Ed's concerns before moving on with the read-aloud. I asked Ed why he felt it was important for us all to be the same. He told me, "If we are not the same we won't be treated equally." I then asked the students why it was important for us all to be treated equally. Kenya, an outspoken, intuitive student, shared, "Yes, I think we should all be treated equally because we are all human beings." The other students put their thumbs up in agreement. I also verbally agreed with Kenya's statement. I then asked Peter if he enjoyed being Chinese and he nodded his head enthusiastically. I posed that same question to each of my students about their own color and culture. Each student revealed how proud he or she was of his or her own cultural background. To bring the conversation back to Ed's original concern, I asked Ed whether he felt comfortable talking about people's cultures in a conversation like this one. Ed smiled and said, "I just didn't want to make anyone feel bad." I responded by conveying my understanding of his concern and explained that this awareness is part of what makes him a compassionate member of our community. "It is the differences that you see and the ones you cannot see with your eyes that make each of us sitting in this room special and interesting." I said. We then resumed the read-aloud. As a result of this conversation students were engaged and actively taking social action by encouraging the acceptance and appreciation of cultures different from our own. While did not anticipate that the classroom read-aloud would begin with such an in-depth conversation, the dialogue during and in response to the book reading was far richer and more memorable than originally planned.

Open conversations such as the above example demonstrate a community which is not only risk-free but also one in which students are, themselves, empowered and able to empower one another to work through issues and address concerns collectively. Adults assume that topics of race and culture are too complex for children to understand. However, it is the opposite for children; their openness allows them to have definitive conversations that adults are uncomfortable with. In our classroom, we felt it would best serve the students creativity and problem-solving skills by actively addressing those issues, which may be considered "scary" for children but will certainly be prevalent throughout their lives.

ACTION

No matter where a student's life leads them, practical problem-solving skills will serve them far longer than "knowledge and recall." With a strong community in place, as a class we began to employ higher-level thinking while working together as problem solvers for social action. For example, questions such as "How can we raise money to send to the hurricane victims?" or "How can we resolve this ongoing conflict between two members of our classroom community?" encourage students to expand their thinking.

In September of 2005–2006, the country was dealing with the aftermath of Hurricane Katrina. As a class we discussed natural catastrophes and, in particular, Hurricane Katrina. Essential questions included: "Who were the victims?"; "What were the victims' experiences?"; "What contributed to the severity of the storm?"; "How could it have been prevented or lessened in damage?"; and "What are things as a community we can do to address the issue?" The students were devastated by the government's slow response to the critical needs of the victims, especially victims residing in lower income areas. The class initiated a school-wide campaign where they were able to collect toiletries, bottled water, clothing, and other relief aid from the larger school community for the hurricane victims. Items were collected and separated by the students, and driven down by my co-teacher to New Orleans. The students later received thank-you notes from the people who benefited from their efforts.

This was the first important lesson in the power of action. Students' concerns and subsequent responses to the catastrophe became the catalyst for action-based learning units by working together and supporting one another in a collective goal to take action; students were empowered and understood their ability to take action. The class community realized that the government was procrastinating about taking action. This realization gave birth to the idea that the students, as citizens, could take action on their own. The students now had an entry point to become agents of change.

As a result of their work, children considered themselves to be the type of people who are fair and just. This worked to our advantage when dealing with classroom management issues. "So let me understand this, we just had a long conversation about helping those in need and you refuse to share a pencil with someone in our own community?" This demonstrates to students the ideas that if we cannot take care of one another within our own community, how are we supposed to create change in the world around us? Often times students were able to reflect and adjust their behavior within the classroom to match their words, aspirations, and actions for the larger societal context.

THE JOURNEY

The stage was now set for the students to embark on a social issues writing unit. It was important for the students to synthesize the knowledge they had acquired through community discussions into a project of their own creation. Working alongside Columbia University's Teachers College for Professional Development, we realized that they did not yet have a fully developed unit, and therefore together as teachers and students we embarked on the journey of creating this unit. As with everything else we began with a conversation. Through a two-month unit entitled Social Issues Unit, students pinpointed issues that concerned them. The concerns ranged from New York City's homeless population, to racism, to the environment. Students went on to research their issue and choose which format was best suited to get their message out. The end products were songs, commercials, and speeches—which were shared with parents and the school community during a performance celebration in the classroom.

During a readers' workshop, students were then exposed to famous speeches, songs, and commercials that dealt with social issues. We read and listened to speeches by famous makers of change such as Martin Luther King Jr., Susan B. Anthony, and Oprah Winfrey. We listened to songs created to heighten social awareness by artists such as Peter Paul and Mary, Paul Simon and Stevie Wonder. We began with a low risk assignment (typically a short-term writing piece that is not used for formal assessment during reading and writing workshops). Through the low-risk writing, students were given artistic leeway to explore their creative writing voices without fear of criticism and to familiarize themselves with different social issues and forms of expressions. Below are several examples of the low-risk assignments.

A.   After reading Oprah Winfrey's Humanitarian Award acceptance speech, students were asked to respond to the following question: You have been given a humanitarian award; write your acceptance speech.

B.   After listening to Peter, Paul and Mary's "If I Had a Hammer," students were asked to create their own songs using original beats. Students developed contemporary beats to a song which is dated but whose message is current.

C. After reading a Susan B. Anthony speech, students were asked to write a letter to their children from the perspective of Susan B. Anthony in jail.

D. After listening to Paul Simon's "My Little Town," students were asked to imagine what their own "little town" would be like if all of the people aged 18–25 were sent off to war.

E. After reading and listening to Martin Luther King Jr.'s "I Have A Dream" speech, students were asked to describe the scene and their experience as if they were in attendance.

SAMPLE OF STUDENT WORK

The biracial student mentioned earlier in the chapter wrote the piece below. His writing is a testament to his own growth in relation to his biracial identity. Kyle stated:

> My black heroes are here for a promise. History is an important thing. When a shot of a gun hits me, Martin prays. I think about him day by day. These are one of Martin's big words, "Hate cannot drive out hate, only love can do that." The world is not a gun or hatred, it's peace and happiness and love. When I hear the words of the past I think of Martin. Martin is my hero and he's yours too. Blacks and whites may not look alike but we are all made of peace.

SOCIAL JUSTICE LESSON

Upon completion of the low-risk writing exploration, students began working on their individual social action pieces. We explored the many different ways to bring about social change. Students were asked the following essential questions: While there are many different ways to reach your audience, what is it you want your audience to walk away with? What do you want them to do with the information? We brainstormed as a classroom a list of problems and issues we saw in the world around us. This list included poverty, environment, racism, diseases, as well as other issues. Once the list was created students separated themselves into groups of interest. What was the issue that was compelling to them based on the research we did together in class? Through that research students found that with all global issues, there was possibility for local action. What change do you want to see in the world around you?

1. Brainstorm a list of social issues. During this session, a safe environment in which all students feel their voices are heard is critical. This conversation took place in a circle, where I jotted down student ideas on chart paper. Afterwards, we took a minute to reflect on what this list meant to us. We then talked about actions we could take in response to these issues, as well as our hopes, for those things that are too large for a classroom to solve. I then asked students what they thought the world would look like 20 years from now. One student said, "I hope that this whole list of all of these problems, no longer exists."

2. Pinpoint the issue that concerns you most. The next day we re-visited the list, discussing each of the topics in order to articulate the issues for students. Students then sat and reflected upon which issue was most important to them. Which issue do you have the most to say about? Which issue do you have the strongest reaction to?

3. Research the topic. Using the internet to share songs and speeches during the research period, my co-teacher and I exposed them to as many different forms of expression dealing with social issues. We took famous and historic speeches and songs and created short extension activities to explore the context of the texts.

4. Decide which format is most effective to disseminate information. Once we explored within activity speeches, songs and commercials, students had to decide which format would be most effective in achieving their goal. Therefore we had to answer several questions. Who is your audience? What are you trying to say? What action do you want people to take as a result of your work? What do you want the end outcome to be? Once students had answered these questions, they then decided what their method would be: commercials, songs, or speeches.

5. Draft. Students worked in groups of mixed topics, employing the same methodology for each topic. The commercial group created storyboards. The speech group drafted speeches. The song group began with poetry. Students worked in free-form partnerships in order to help one another through the process. They were able to enjoy freedom throughout this process, as a result of the community environment that had been developing throughout the year.

6. Revise. Students assisted each other through the revision process by pointing out areas that required further development and editing.

7. Edit. With the assistance of my co-teacher and me, students edited their work in preparation for presentation.

8. Action. As a vital part of the process, students' concerns are shared with the larger culture and their work becomes action. Students shared commercials,

songs, and speeches with families, administration, and other classes. Students received feedback in the form of letters from other students. Other classes were inspired to learn after viewing the work of my students.

THE RIPPLE EFFECT

The class was able to take action in the form of speech writing, song writing and film (commercial) making. We created a class-wide action-based project. By the end of the school year, our community had taken a collective interest in the environment and global warming. With our guidance, students created useful inventions out of items that would normally be thrown away. As a grade level, we held an auction open to parents and families in the larger school community. Notably, 65 children were able to raise $1,000 in less than two hours. In the days to come, our community came to a consensus and decided to donate the money to Stop Global Warming (an organization dedicated to educating the public on steps we can take to stop the effects of global warming). Our community hosted an assembly in which the students presented a check to the organization and celebrated the environment through dance, poetry, and art. The organization was so impressed with the students' efforts that they put their story on their website and named them as activists. They were able to see their action taking effect in the world.

My experience as a teacher has been a transformative process for my students and myself. This class began with a group of diverse learners who, with the support of my co-teacher and me, were able to form a community. This community was built on the tenets of respect and recognition and celebration of diversity in all forms. Throughout this process we watched students grow in many ways. During the course of the year, students' diversity was not only evident in our classroom; it was a key element in our supporting curriculum. Students of all cultures—which included bilingual/bicultural students—were able to express their own perspectives to others, and widen their scope of experiences and perspectives. The vast social, emotional, economic, racial, and cultural differences were instrumental in forming a cohesive and exciting community. The community's support and recognition were critical to our success in taking social action. When we allow children to see themselves, and claim their voices, they begin to understand that they can create change in the world around them. This understanding transforms students' natural concern and empathy into inspiring action. Action within the framework of social justice creates opportunity for all students' voices to be heard.

In a system driven by standardized tests, educators have a great responsibility. We must remember that we are empowered individuals in the educational process. Teaching is an art form; it is a human experience. Every day, within the four walls of our classrooms, our words and actions leave an indelible mark on our students. Although there are those within the system who are busy at work attempting to create sterile assessment to which teacher and student alike must answer to, we, as teachers know the true social and emotional growth that we see within our students cannot be quantified by any standardized test.

I began my journey as an educator to inspire my students; in the end it was my students who inspired me. Each day I arrived in my classroom, my students taught me about my life, their lives, and the world in which we live together. I quickly learned that it was my job to nurture their curiosities and concerns by creating a framework allowing them to take action and lead the way. What this group of eight- and nine-year-olds accomplished was quite remarkable. At first I thought it was unique to this particular group of compassionate students, but I have realized that these qualities of compassion and justice are inherent in all students. It is our mission as educators to give students the tools and environment necessary to empower themselves.

CHAPTER THIRTEEN

Culture and Language in the Classroom from the Perspective of a Latina Teacher

MERCEDES E. CEPEDA

In the era of No Child Left Behind (NCLB) laws, bilingual/bicultural children face the daunting task of catching up with the American mainstream learners who fluently speak and write in English. Thousands of English Language Learners (ELL), who make up a sizable student population and have not learned the English language, are tested in English. The consequences of this will have a negative effect upon ELL students—who will be subjected to federal mandates and suffer from educational malpractice. Not only is this a relevant problem to classrooms today—given the high rates of bilingual/bicultural student disengagement and lack of motivation—but it will hurt the future of this country by increasing the achievement gap. Standardized exams continue to ignore the needs of ELL students, and many of these students, especially Latino students, eventually drop out of school.

When I decided to become a teacher, one of the first thoughts that I had was that I did not look like the majority of teachers being recruited as a New York City Teaching Fellow—I was not White! The majority of the teachers today recruited in urban centers are young White females and most of the students they teach are non-white. According to the Laird (2007), 40% of the schools are populated by children of color, and 90% of the teachers are White. The lack of Latino (bilingual/bicultural) teachers is not representative of the student population who are bilingual and bicultural. According to the National Collaborative on Diversity in the Teaching Force (2004), the number of students of color is increasing in the United

States, while the availability of teachers of color is not increasing to meet the needs of a diverse teaching force. For example, in the Los Angeles County, California, Latino students make up over 60% of the K-12 population yet only 14% of employed teachers are Latino teachers. My experience and global awareness leads me to expect the above statistics to be rising.

MY EXPERIENCE AS A LATINA TEACHER

I do not exemplify what most people think about when they think of a reading and writing teacher. I have been confused for the Spanish teacher, the social studies teacher or even the math teacher. But looking at my students' progress when they complete their classroom writing assignments is enough indication that I am a successful English teacher. Additionally, the fact that my students—who were labeled as the weakest performing class—were among the highest performing group of students on the ELA exams in the school is also an indicator that my instruction is creating academically successful students.

I believe that anyone can teach the material that I am teaching but not everyone can create a caring classroom, a classroom built around academic success, and culturally relevant instruction that will motivate the students. This ability needs to come from teachers' will and passion to want a better life for the students.

Culturally relevant teaching embraces culture and language in the classroom. When speaking to my students I often have to articulate "well it is like this in Spanish" and they immediately understand what I am communicating to them. Bilingual people process information in both English and Spanish. For example, while I do not speak Spanish as often as I do English, I calculate numbers in Spanish. I am particularly challenged by my Saturday reading and writing tutorial class—consisting of Asian students. My biggest challenge is creating a connection with them that fosters true comprehension and appreciation of the material. One day the class was working on inserting details in writing. I told the students that instead of writing "I ate dinner," they could write, "I had one of my favorite dishes last night. My mother prepared rice, beans, and plantains." It took me around 15 minutes to explain to them what plantains were and why I was not eating tacos. The students had difficulty relating to the culture that I bring to the classroom. What they know of Latinas is what they are exposed to on television and, perhaps, from the scarce interaction with the Latino community in their primarily Asian communities.

Moreover, when Asian parents come in to speak to me and realize that I am not Asian, nor do I understand their language, they stay away from the classroom. This creates a disconnect between what is happening in the classroom and their lives.

This is not an effective classroom culture for me. I ask how someone who cares about effective education cannot address these issues of isolation, disconnection, and culturally relevant instruction. As part of the American community, we often have racial and ethnic biases which also pervade the educational communities. As educators, it's important to engage in discussion on this matter.

During staff meetings I often rehearse what I will say and how I will say it. If I speak Spanish to a colleague it is as if I am acting outside of the norm for a teacher who does not teach Spanish. I was once told by our grade team leader "that language is not used in here." He smiled to imply that he was joking, but I questioned what part of him was not joking. Did he think that speaking Spanish was inappropriate or not good enough? At that moment I felt like I was using profanity in front of the teacher. Teachers should be asked what they think a teacher looks like and confront their personal biases about teachers, not just students—as they often discuss their personal biases of students in professional settings. Moreover, a skill that is often discouraged by conservative teachers is very gratifying to me. I am no longer the assistant (as many students become translators for their parents) translating to another teacher during a parent-teacher conference; I am the teacher that can communicate to my student's parents without a translator and therefore teaching for and in the 21st century. Communicating with the parents in their native language gives you so much more insight into who the student is. During parent-teacher conferences the students, parents and myself all talk in Spanish, which allows the conversation to grow outside of the meeting. Students are more responsive when they know you can speak directly to their parents. The relationship that grows from communicating with your students' parents can foster academic success.

In my classroom we try to find a common ground between the languages we use and who we are; we choose to maintain our Latino bilingual and bicultural identity. The use of standardized English can at times discourage students from participating in classroom discussions especially when teachers are insensitive to language barriers and immediately correct the language of their students. In *Other People's Children* (1995), Lisa Delpit argues that many children of color feel that speaking standardized English is talking or acting "White." On the other hand, some teachers are more concerned with correcting the "nonstandardized" language of many children of color. I tell my students that speaking Standard English does not mean that you are acting "White," and that there is a time and place for every form of speech.

Teachers can confer with their students and have discussions about who they are. I ask students to talk about their favorite food, or discuss a trip back to their country; I ask questions to make them comfortable about who they are, proud of their culture, and talk with confidence. We start with small group conferences because dialogue about your personal life can be intense. After we have built a sense of trust and are comfortable with the idea of talking in front of a small group, then we move on to larger classroom discussions often about our great diversity.

The best moments come when students ask questions about each other's cultures and traditions—needing very little facilitation. During one of the lessons, a student shouted that he was not an immigrant but he was American. My response was, oh that's great, well I am an immigrant and I love going back to the Dominican Republic. After the writing period was over he wanted to share with the class why he loves going back home to his country. At this moment any stereotypes or negative feelings he had about his identity started to dismantle.

Our students should enjoy going to school. As teachers we need to feel comfortable and enjoy what we are doing, students feed off our energy. I teach students that if you love what you do you will do well. Bicultural/bilingual students really need to be able to connect with and respect what teachers are teaching. When teachers bring what they are familiar with, we create a successful environment in the classroom. For instance, one of my students was always disruptive during reading and writing. I asked the counselor to sit in, I contacted the parents, set meetings up with the appropriate people, and one day I decided to ask him what was going on in his head when he was in class. He said "I am bored." I had spent a lot of time in thought about him so I was ready to have a conversation and listen to what he had to say. Sometimes teachers ask students questions but we are not ready to hear the response. I asked him what he found interesting and what he liked. He told me he loved football, and his brother and Malcolm X. I tried really hard to get him what he liked and he did very well. His disruptive behavior improved, he was disruptive when he wanted attention just like any other student, but it helped tremendously when he was able to read the books of his liking and write about his brother and things that mattered to him.

A teacher's job has never been easy; the education system has never empathized with bilingual/bicultural children. It needs to realize that in order to teach bilingual/bicultural students effectively, we need to understand their norms that will enable us to engage, motivate, and connect with bilingual/bicultural students. Schools must understand where bilingual/bicultural students come from, their prior knowledge, and that their needs are based on diverse variables. A culturally relevant teacher's instruction is centered on the students' cultural needs, language, and identity that empowers the classroom community and will foster a community of learners who will feel connected to the education that they are receiving. This will eventually help close the achievement gap and deal with dropout rates, low standardized testing scores, violence in schools, classroom management, low attendance rate and other struggles that schools are currently facing.

Teachers need to become researchers—research the world, the community, the students, and themselves. With all the information and resources available to us as teachers, change is inevitable because the knowledge that one acquires through researching, putting our research into practice, will ultimately influence students. This will drive and inspire us as teachers to keep updating and changing our practices which will best suit the students' needs.

SUGGESTIONS FOR CREATING A CARING CLASSROOM

1. Get to know the students and their culture, especially on the first few days of school. Seamlessly tell them about yourself and really learn about the students. Focus lessons on who they are.
2. Monday morning meetings: Students can write you a letter and you should respond. Communication is the best way for great classroom relationships and success.
3. Call all parents, introduce parents to each other, and maintain a relationship through calls and invitations to the classroom. Talk to the parents or guardians in Spanish if you can, be honest with your Spanish, do not standardize it. By this I mean use your accent and dialect. Be aware and understand the Spanish hierarchy. Be professional but be yourself.
4. Be consistent with discipline and instruction. Use what is natural to you, if what you learned in school works for you and your students use it. However, every year this changes. The best strategies come if they are natural and familiar to you.
5. Verbally let the students know why you do things. There should not be any surprises. The students will respect you if you are clear about everything that you do. Keep an agenda and stick to it. Also let students know what choices they made and what consequences those choices have.
6. Use positive reinforcement daily. Most students do not get this at home. My students hardly ever get a nice job from their parents, it means the world to them when you can call their parents and tell them how great they are in the classroom.
7. Cooperative learning/diverse teaching methods. The students learn more from each other then they do from a lecture. Bring life into your teaching, by introducing different approaches. The more the students speak the better. Model to them how to work in groups; the chaos comes when the procedures and expectations are not clear.
8. Student affirmation of each other. When students compliment each other, they go from children to young adults. Teach them this skill and you will

be a successful teacher.

9. I've learned that one-on-one time with students goes a long way, even if it's a five-minute review, conversation, or personal lesson to review or to advance the student.

Teachers learn from research and practical experience. They both go hand in hand and cannot exist without each other. Many teachers would be better prepared if their teacher preparation courses in college taught how to serve bilingual and bicultural children. Many teachers would be better prepared to teach in predominately non-white schools if they were instructed in culturally relevant curricula coursework. While workshops and seminars give us an idea of this material, teachers need to immerse themselves in culturally relevant teaching courses that will give them the tools to be successful in the classroom.

Additionally, students need to be empowered in order to feel motivated to participate equitably in the classroom. The goal is to bring social justice and equitable opportunities into the classroom so that bicultural/bilingual students will have the same opportunity to succeed as any other student. The above steps have worked for me and have created a trusting environment. They have helped me as a teacher and allowed me to get to know students at a faster pace. I teach with a simple goal—I want my students to learn and to be successful. Therefore, I weave my passion and my sincerity into my pedagogy.

FINAL THOUGHTS

Working with bicultural/bilingual students is a great opportunity to really embrace community teaching and community learning. Not only does the student benefit from having a teacher who is similar to them in many ways, teachers also bring culture, traditions, habits, etc. from our cultures that impact the students. In turn, we have more to give and more to inspire our teaching than just our teaching styles or skills. Our connection and impact are so magnificent that the energy in a classroom is unbelievable. We can teach the curriculum but we can also teach habits, history, and culture, and inspire many to be successful in life. The student population is changing rapidly; each year in all my classes the number of incoming Latino students and bilingual students increases and I am aware that the students feel happy when their teacher and advisor can speak Spanish to their parents and can have a greater connection with the students and their families.

Being a bicultural/bilingual teacher is a great advantage. I listen to and understand my bicultural/bilingual students but I also am aware of the choices that they need to make in order to become successful citizens of this world. As teachers every day we see the future in our classrooms looking at us, students look at us for answers; it's our job to give them honest and true answers that come from true experiences. I teach the curriculum and meet the standards; yet I teach students that it is okay to be who they are; I teach students to feel comfortable and successful in this multicultural world. Lastly, I continue to build on my experiences and knowledge by actively researching in order to understand the world and create change. It's about knowing who you are and being yourself in the classroom and students will grow and respect you.

CHAPTER FOURTEEN

Teachers Overcoming Silence

SHARON L. HIXON

In many societal systems, there exist hegemonic practices. People in power are able to maintain domination and oppress the voices of minorities. This often takes place in order to maintain the status quo. We call this practice silencing. Teachers are often cited as culprits in these acts of silencing. However, teachers themselves can be victims of silencing. Teachers and other educational professionals can take active steps to bring forth their voices and the voices of other oppressed people (Asher, 2007; Cammarota & Romero, 2006; Chapman, 2007; Copenhaver-Johnson, Bowman, & Johnson, 2007; Dalley-Trim, 2006; Duncan-Owens, 2008).

In essence, teachers can encourage students' voices to be heard by serving as active listeners for their students (Taylor et al., 1995), by providing forums in the classroom that allow for authentic discussions about gender, race and power (Cammarota & Romero, 2006; Copenhaver-Johnson et al., 2007), by being self-reflective on issues of race, power, and stereotypes (Asher, 2007; Dalley-Trim, 2006; Jackson, 1999), by utilizing instructional strategies that connect the cultural backgrounds of the children to the content being taught and that insure the group work is empowering (Lopez & Hall, 2007; Matthews & Kesner, 2000; Schneider, 2001), and by developing their own research agendas (Llorens, 1994).

NO CHILD LEFT BEHIND

Without a doubt, the No Child Left Behind Act (NCLBA) has effectively silenced teachers by disallowing them a voice in curriculum decisions and in the selection of teaching practices. Firstly, Duncan-Owens (2008) suggests that NCLBA has left teachers voiceless when it comes to issues of instruction. Teachers are seen as simple vehicles to dispense pre-designed and pre-packed curricula. Teachers are given little or no voice in deciding which reading program to use, or even how to use the programs chosen by others. Duncan-Owens (2008) refers to this as "fidelity of implementation" (p. 15). In other words, the robotic distributor of the curriculum is to follow the program without question, without regard to his/her training, and without regard to specific needs children in the classroom may have. Duncan-Owens believes that it may take up to three years of program usage before teachers are given a chance to voice concerns on a reading program. She reminds us that this could mean we may have had three years of "wasted time, wasted evidence, and wasted resources" (p. 15). Chapman (2007) also sheds light on how a teacher's decision making processes are invalidated through the NCLBA's use of the terms best practices and interventions (p. 26). Chapman argues this implies that teachers are "technicians" that utilize "ready-made solutions for transmitting knowledge" (p. 26).

Cammarota and Romero (2006) focus on the NCLBA's impact on students mirroring the conclusions drawn by Chapman and Duncan-Owens. Cammarota and Romero also suggest that the focus on "high stakes testing" has indeed led teachers to see themselves as transmitters of knowledge and has caused them to be concerned "with only the technical (i.e., skill level) side of their student's experiences" rather than to exhibit "authentic caring" or the ability to show that the teacher has "a real interest with the students' overall wellbeing" (p. 21).

Some believe that the NCLBA has been an effective method for silencing the voices of teachers, Llorens (1994) found that even when teachers were provided with opportunities to conduct action research, they often "lacked a sense of their own voice and its importance to educational improvement in their own classrooms" (p.6).

SILENCING INSTRUCTIONAL AIDES

Esquivel and his associates (2002) remind educators that instructional aides are also often silenced—as they are not even part of the equation of school reform decisions. The authors suggest that specific children may find themselves spending a larger portion of their day with the instructional aides than they do with the classroom teacher. In addition, Esquivel and his associates suggest that in some school districts the ethnic backgrounds of the aides may be more representative of the community than one will find in the ethnic backgrounds of the teachers. If one takes into consideration the amount of time the children spend with the instructional aid, and the idea that the instructional aides may have a more similar ethnic background to the children they serve, then it seems illogical to silence their voices as school reform decisions are developed and implemented.

An instructional aide interviewed in the research of Esquivel and his associates compared children in the classroom where she worked to her own children. Olinthia, the aide, felt as if she communicated that she cared about them while some of the classroom teachers "othered" the students of different ethnicities/races. If the school reform movements do not explicitly consider "race, class, and gender" (p. 217), then the voices of the instructional aides may continue to be silenced. This is problematic because we need their special expertise and knowledge of the children as the decision-making process of school reform is undertaken. They may be able to offer insights that various teachers and administrators may not have.

SILENCING CULTURALLY DIVERSE CHILDREN

Children from diverse minority groups all around the world are silenced in a myriad of ways; some of them are deliberately silenced by oppressors while others are silenced through good intentions, or institutionalized racism, or sexism. Female children are effectively silenced; often the boys in the classroom silence the girls by calling attention to the girls' physical selves. The boys can silence the girls by commanding them to be silent, or the girls can choose to be silent because they see this as a method to gain acceptance into the group (Dalley-Trim, 2006; Taylor, et al., 1995).

Children who come from cultures different from the mainstream culture can be silenced because they operate from different world views and may learn or demonstrate knowledge in a manner that is unfamiliar or unacceptable to the mainstream teachers. Children with learning differences can be silenced when they are required to work in cooperative groups. This can happen because the children in the cooperative group are trying to help or because they are deliberately ignoring the contributions of the child with learning differences. Topics ranging from racism to homosexuality are silenced in classrooms. Sometimes, the silencing of these topics can lead to the silencing of the child's culture, as happens with Dustin (a pseudonym) in the Kendrick and Mckay, 2002 study. Dustin felt as if he could not write about his deer-hunting experiences in his class writing assignments because topics that dealt with violence were forbidden in the classroom (Benham & Heck, 1998; Copenhaver-Johnson et al., 2007; Hankins, 1999; Lopez & Hall, 2007; Matthews & Kesner, 2000; Schneider, 2001; Taylor, et al., 1995).

STRATEGIES FOR TEACHERS

Silencing is an insidious tool used to help the powerful retain their power. As such, there is no single suggestion that bilingual/bicultural educators can use to help the voiceless find their voices or to provide safe spaces for their voices to be heard. Despite this fact, there are plenty of strategies that can be employed.

For girls, having women who listen, hear, and share may be a key to providing "a safety net" (Taylor et al., 1995). For example, the adolescent girls in the Taylor study who had "a resonant relationship with a woman" (p. 4) who actually listened to them and shared her own stories were less likely to make choices that led to teen pregnancy or dropping out of school and were more likely to graduate and continue on to college or a working environment. Demonstrating "authentic caring" (Cammarota & Romero, 2006, p. 21) resonates in other studies as well. At least one of the teens in the Cammarota and Romero study suggested that the students would be more likely to open up with honest communication if the researchers/instructors shared their own experiences

For teachers who use cooperative learning activities in the classroom, Matthews and Kesner (2000) offer ways to improve the "dynamics at work within these groups" (p. 388). In their minds, students like Sammy (a child with learning differences silenced by cooperative group work) may have more opportunities to have their voices heard if there are fewer students in the cooperative groups, if the students have been properly trained to work in cooperative groups, if the teacher uses observation and measurement tools to better understand each child's status amongst his/her peers, and if the teacher uses methods "to change the social order in the classroom" (p. 388). In other words, the teacher will train the students for group work in such a way that hierarchical power and silencing will not be allowed.

Teachers who encourage conversations about race and power may want to consider what Copenhaver-Johnson et al.(2007) have found effective. First, teachers will need to foster a safe classroom environment that allows discussion of race. Next, teachers, themselves, will need to find ways to make themselves more at ease when discussing race issues. In essence, they have to have these conversations frequently in order to hone their abilities to use caring methods to let children know that the teacher has a divergent point of view. They will need to find ways to identify which voices are not being heard in the classroom and which voices are being heard. After they understand who is and is not being heard, the teachers need to develop questions or other methods to promote the silenced children's voices.

In addition, conversations about race and power can be enhanced by utilizing children's books that include racism as part of the context of the book. If children are indeed forming their own ideas about race and its connection to power differentials (as did the first grade children in the Copenhaver-Johnson et al. study), then it is important for elementary teachers to ensure these conversations about race are not silenced. If these conversations are silenced, then teachers run the risk of children forming their impressions with limited background knowledge. Often, this background knowledge relies on their own limited experiences with people of races other than their own.

In order for teachers to foster discussions on race and power in the classroom, they must first be given a safe place to have their own conversations about such topics. Jackson (1999) advocates that White teacher-candidates be given plenty of opportunities to examine any "dysconscious racist behaviors" (p. 17) they may exhibit. In other words, she wants them to examine their assumptions about race and class. White teacher-candidates need to wrestle with the ideas that such beliefs may perpetuate racism. At the same time, African American teacher-candidates need safe places "to engage in the process of unlearning internalized racism" (p. 17). In other words, she wants these students to wrestle with the idea that they may have internalized racist ideas that suggest that they are somehow unworthy or incapable of acquiring an education or that they must assimilate into mainstream culture in order to receive such an education. In essence, teacher-candidates need to examine their own belief systems regarding race in a safe environment before they can begin to engage elementary students in the process of discussing race and power (Asher, 2007; Jackson, 1999).

Asher (2007) feels it is important for teacher-candidates to reflect upon the "context-specific intersections of race, class, gender, sexuality, culture, and language" (p. 67). In other words, Asher does not advocate pre-service multicultural education classes that take each of the above-mentioned conditions and look at them as separate entities. In other words, it would make no sense for a college professor to address issues of gender (for instance) as a separate entity effecting one's life. In Asher's view, an individual who is both Latina and female, for example, is affected by her race and gender simultaneously. The teacher-candidate needs the opportunity offered by a teacher-trainer who establishes a safe classroom environment to raise his/her "contradictions, doubts, and questions" (p. 71) about the intersections previously mentioned. Thus, Jackson and Asher seem to agree that part of the responsibility for the ratification of silencing lies in the hand of the teacher-trainers who are working with pre-service teachers.

Another way teachers can help eliminate silencing is to become aware of stereotypes they themselves hold and how these stereotypes may foster silencing practices in the classroom. For example, if teachers see gender or ethnic background from an "essentialist" (Dalley-Trim, 2006, p. 30) point of view, then they can help to perpetuate these stereotypes and the silences that they bring. In other words, because teachers may subscribe to the belief that "boys will be boys" they are less likely to have " problematised (sic)" (p. 26) the behavior. In essence, they will see the behavior as acceptable for boys and not attempt to find ways to help boys to construct a masculine identity that is "less disenfranchising to their female peers" (Dalley-Trim, 2006, p. 32).

One way teachers can learn about the stereotypes they hold is through self-reflection. Jackson (1999) suggests that teacher candidates need to have activities in their classes that guide them through such reflections, so teacher-trainers are an important element in helping to validate the voices of all. Jackson (1999) and Schneider (2001) call upon teachers to look at their belief systems; in other words, teachers must identify and acknowledge the biases they hold, and they must make conscious decisions to evaluate the manner in which these biases impact instructional choices and daily exchanges with their students.

Children's voices can also be heard or be recognized when educators find ways to connect a student's cultural heritage with the topic at hand. Lopez and Hall (2007) discuss the National Indian Youth Leadership Project (NIYLP) that used grant money to run programs for the Diné children in the summer, on Saturdays, and after school. These programs found a myriad of ways to link the students' cultural backgrounds to academic learning. Through singing, dancing, weaving, and painting of murals (for instance), "children were able to demonstrate what they already knew about the world even though it may have been a world of his/her People and not of the mainstream" (p. 33).

Esquivel and his associates (2002) believe that we are living in a world that continues to perpetuate the myth of a "color-blind, race-neutral democracy." Availing ourselves of this ideology allows the perpetuation of the "status quo" (p. 207), and thus, the voices of many continue to be unheard. Esquivel and his associates argue that we cannot possibly help the silenced voices be heard until we meet the first stage of Freire's vision. In other words, they believe that educators must find ways to bring the racist systems to light if we ever want to find ways to educate the oppressors, the second stage of Freire's vision. Esquivel and his associates suggest using narratives as one method for bringing issues of "race, class, and gender" (p. 216) to the forefront of policy discussion and decisions.

Cammarota and Romero (2006) argue that teachers who believe in and follow the pedagogy of "critically compassionate intellectualism" "will provide their students with the opportunity to counter the institutional silencing that prevents their full and active participation in shaping their futures" (p. 18). Cammarota and Romero promote the idea that teachers must include in their belief systems and in their pedagogical strategies a way for students to engage with discussions that bring to light instances of oppression that are foisted upon them and followed without question. They also must develop instructional strategies that afford students the opportunity to make decisions about what is learned, how it might be learned, and what they can do to make changes in society. In other words, students need to be engaged in learning relevant to their learning styles and relevant to their knowledge base. Finally, the teachers must be open with their students, so their students can trust them and feel comfortable becoming co-constructors of the information learned. While Cammarota and Romero studied Latino/a teenagers and developed their ideas to be applied to the teaching of Latino/a teens, a teacher does not have to wait until children have blossomed into adolescence before ideas of oppression, racism, and the like are discussed in the classroom.

Besides having discussions on issues of race and power, teachers can provide opportunities for students' voices when they create their writing instruction and when they provide feedback to students' writings. Schneider (2001) suggests that teachers must develop a writing program that affords students the opportunity for "individual and group freedom of expression." Teachers can pave the way for this freedom in their classroom if they are willing "to provide students with the time to write on topics of their choice, in genres of their choice, without fear of criticism, exposure, or grades" (p. 423). When the children share their writing, it is totally possible that this will stimulate more of the discussions that will build the "critically compassionate intellectualism" (p. 18) that Cammarota and Romero advocate. Regardless of the method of writing instruction chosen, Schneider advocates a writing program that does not use redirecting. In other words, teachers should not be asking students to write about the "sunny days" (Dustin as cited in Kendrick & McKay, 2002, p. 52) that were so disturbing to Dustin in the Kendrick McKay study. Schneider also suggests teachers will need to be prepared to handle topics that may stimulate uncomfortable feelings in themselves, and they will need to have a well-developed plan for how they might use critical thinking instead of avoidance when these topics occur in children's writing and in their sharing of the writing.

Conclusion

Silencing is neither easily labeled nor easily rectified. If the teaching community wishes to hear and recognize the voices of all, then we must work together to recognize our own biases. Identifying and recognizing our own biases will not be a comfortable process for many. Teachers and teacher candidates will be better prepared to do this reflective work if the teacher–trainers provide the safe environments that begin the discussions about marginalized voices, marginalized topics, and marginalized cultures. Once these teachers have had the opportunity to reflect, then they should be more prepared to incorporate practices in their school classrooms that will allow children to discuss the often silenced topics and will afford children the opportunities to meet with academic success without giving up their own cultural beliefs or ways of knowing. If we want all children to meet with success in our classrooms, then all of us must first know where our biases are located. Then, we must work diligently to make sure our own voices are not silenced. Next, we must make sure the voices of all of our students are heard. Finally, we must realize that we cannot engage in the reflective work once and then change our classrooms overnight. Instead, we must be continuously vigilant and reflective and encourage this same behavior in our colleagues and students. In the end, this effort to end silencing can lead to academic success and end the hegemonic practices that allow the powerful to maintain the status quo.

CHAPTER FIFTEEN

Learning for Children's and Teachers' Stories

Elizabeth P. Quintero

Many children and their teachers today in schools have exquisitely complex stories of going and coming. They have gone from a home country for a myriad of reasons, and they have come to their new country with a multitude of experiences. Making language and culture visible through multicultural literacy is crucial for immigrant students in school. This can and must be in the context of standardized curriculum requirements. This chapter highlights several early childhood classrooms in which many children came to the United States from another country. The student teachers designing and implementing the lessons were themselves from immigrant families and were committed to using critical literacy as a way to build upon the strengths of families' cultural history and use the information in the daily curriculum.

> We live today with multiple representations, some we call science, some we call art, precise, abstract, vivid, and evocative, each one proposing new connections....Human beings construct meanings as spiders make webs—or as appropriate enzymes make proteins. This is how we survive (Bateson, 1997, p. 52).

MULTIPLE REPRESENTATIONS—WHY STORIES?

Telling our own stories is intricately related to survival. We construct meanings as spiders make webs. And surviving is a complex task. There is physical survival. There is emotional survival. And, of course, there is historical and cultural survival. It may be that the only way to delve into survival is through personal story. In many ways, we are all responsible for being microhistorians. We are equally responsible to pay attention to the microhistories of others:

> We all have our biases and limited viewpoints. It all depends on where we stand. Microhistorians, I think, are just a little more honest about it. We tend to believe that there is no such thing as a definitive History—only a series of micro histories (Romo, 2005, p. 18).

Children and their teachers, in my experience, are natural microhistorians.

Novelists, artists, and visionaries have relied on the importance of story for centuries. Rymes (2001) documents her "field work in educational borderlands" (p. 12) and acknowledges that storytelling saves many an educational activity. I believe that story makes the connection between the identity and the history of participants and the educational programs of study. Sfard and Prusak (2005) say, "We believe that the notion of identity is a perfect candidate for the role of 'the missing link' in the researchers' story of the complex dialect between learning and its sociocultural context" (p. 15).

Story is a way to make language and culture visible through multicultural literacy events. This is crucial for all learners and especially for immigrant students in school. To belong is to be recognized as a full participant in the practices that shape knowledge, identities, and action. Yet to learn is to draw upon one's own and others' knowledge sources, to transform these, and formulate conceptual frames for future learning. Urban neighborhoods and schools have increasing numbers of people representing ethnic, racial, and religious diversity. Many students today in schools around our country have exquisitely complex stories of going and coming. They have gone from a home country for a myriad of reasons, and they have come to their new country with a multitude of experiences. The experts in our newest refugee and immigrant neighborhoods have much to teach other students, other families, and educators. Teachers and students can use multicultural story and critical literacy as a way to enter neighborhoods and begin to learn from other stories of the various groups of people. Furthermore, the study of our students' histories must be on-going and a part of literacy education.

I work with groups of student-teachers in urban and rural schools in diverse communities in several states. I and the teachers I work with support students' multiple languages and recognize ways that multiple knowledge sources, identities, and language forms can contribute to the formation of new relationships and meanings. As a community of scholars in a wide variety of classrooms, we respect the children's backgrounds, plan carefully for their current experiences in school, and prepare them for the future challenges of standardized testing, competitive learning programs, and a variety of future journeys. Our work uses critical literacy as a framework. We define critical literacy as a process of constructing and critically using language (oral and written) as a means of expression, interpretation and/or transformation of our lives and the lives of those around us.

Our work uses critical literacy as a framework for integrated curriculum that includes all the traditional content areas of study—the arts and new forms of cross-disciplinary ways of knowing. By using a problem-posing, critical literacy approach with multicultural children's literature and the words of many community members who are not currently "heard," this environment of possibility is optimized for students.

The excerpts presented here are part of a qualitative study documenting teacher education students in their student teaching experiences as they create critical literacy activities and curriculum for children in kindergarten, first, and second grade classrooms. The methods of data collection involved participant observation, interviews, teacher journals, and collection of learners' work samples. The data was analyzed by categories that are emphasized in critical theory: (a) the importance of personal history and culture of all participants, (b) the recognition of multiple sources of knowledge, and (c) transformative action.

Our research questions based upon critical literacy were: Whose stories are important and in what ways? What ways can we learn from the stories? Whose background knowledge will we respect and include and in what ways? Whose and which knowledge is power and in what ways? What ways can we use literacy for specific transformative action?

PERSONALIZING STORIES AND YOUNG CHILDREN'S LEARNING

The contemporary poet Francisco X. Alarcón asks us if we can "hear the voices between these lines?" (1997: 28) The personal voices of teachers, of students, of friends in our communities around the world are the voices we hear between the lines in all literacy events. For this reason, when I speak of literacy, all literacy is—or should be literacy. This constructing of personal and communal meaning and taking action according to the meaning is the most authentic way to personalize literacy. Our cultural human roots that we pass on to children are no longer neatly contained within borders. According to Clandinin and Connelly (1996), the act of our telling our stories seems "inextricably linked with the act of making meaning, an inevitable part of life in a...postmodern world" and only becomes problematic "when its influence on thinking and perception goes unnoticed," or is ignored (Goldstein, 1997, p. 147)

Moll, Gonzalez, and Amanti (2005) give long-awaited documentation to the theoretical and practical issues of Funds of Knowledge as important contributions to our knowledge in the various fields of education. The research presented here in this chapter addresses the funds of knowledge of educators (families and community members) in a diverse context of a variety of cultures and situations of living. It is through the use of critical theory and critical literacy that the histories, languages, and multiple forms of knowledge from around the world come into our lexicon.

Teachers can show students that their stories are important and learn important information from them in the process. For example, a teacher education student who implemented a critical literacy agenda for a group of kindergarten children was interested in the broad issues of culture and identity (as they relate to language and learning). She commented often that this issue of meaning through language is important to her. Her case reveals aspects of critical theory in the aspects of personal story/history, multiple sources of knowledge, and transformative action with kindergarten students. She wrote in a journal entry:

> *A topic that has been of particular interest to me in early education has been that of responsiveness to family cultures, values and languages. Having immigrated to the United States at a young age with my family, I have a personal connection with this topic. In my opinion, the incorporation of different cultures, values, and languages about each other's likenesses and differences via their culture, values, and language should be a part of all teachers' curricula. Persons who come from different backgrounds can provide one another with new ideas or perspectives otherwise not explored.*

She, as all the examples following from the case studies, used the Listening, Dialogue, Action format often used in critical literacy curriculum.

LISTENING

She read *The Colors of Us* by Karen Katz (2007). The story is about a child whose mother is an artist who insists that there are many different shades of brown. Mother and daughter take a walk through their neighborhood thinking about friends and relatives and the skin colors of all of them. Their skin colors are compared to honey, peanut butter, pizza crust, ginger, peaches, chocolate, and more, conjuring up delicious and beautiful comparisons for every tint.

DIALOGUE

She asked the children, "What did you see or notice about the story?" Then she asked them to talk more about the comparisons the author made about skin color and different foods. She then brought the discussion to the topic of language by asking if the students could say or know about the language a person speaks by looking at skin color.

She then asked the children to explore ideas in the book by asking open-ended questions such as what preferred activities did you see in the book? So the people who like that activity speak only one language? Do people who speak the same language always have the same skin color?

ACTION

Then she read the book *Why ?* by Norma Simon (1993). This book is about some of the things that make us all different and uniquely ourselves. The story invokes opportunities for discussions about the many differences that make people so unique from the way we look, to language, to food, to preferred activities.

For action inside the classroom during choice time, she planned the learning centers as follows:

1. One center was equipped with dress up clothes from different cultures for children. There were also encyclopedias, National Geographic magazines, and a variety of books from UNICEF with pictures of people from a variety of countries and cultures. A labeled world map was displayed in the classroom.
2. At the art center, children could create life-sized outlines and self-portraits of themselves.
3. At a second art table, with partners and in small groups using a variety of art materials, children explored food comparisons for their own skin color. They drew or painted pictures of the food and wrote a few phrases or sentences about this comparison. There was an extension categorization activity that consisted of different fruits and vegetables and the various nutrition facts.
4. At the book center, there were different multicultural books on tape in English and in other languages that groups of children listened to.

For action outside the classroom, she asked children (after sending a letter home to families) to bring in a family artifact—preferably from their kitchens—representing their culture or a certain tradition that they have with their family. She explained that she was also interested in home items that displayed labels or writing of other languages—such as empty food boxes. The children brought the artifacts into class during the next few days and made an "artifact/language/family" exhibit in the classroom.

The student teacher, whose family is from Iran, reported that she learned from the children bringing in artifacts from their homes that two children were from different Middle Eastern countries. During the map activity she learned a little about several students from a variety of countries whose family members still lived in their home countries. Her study of critical theory and critical literacy influenced her frustration with the cooperating teacher's apparent lack of support of transformative action. She wrote:

> *I really wished the teacher did more for R. She speaks Spanish (she is), and she was able to communicate with him when he did not understand what was going on, but that is where her support ended. R.'s family spoke minimal English and they could not read anything she handed out, so he was never able to do the family homework projects or the reading logs. The family asked for the handouts to be translated into Spanish, but the teacher thought that was not her job…I think what upset me the most was that the teacher speaks Spanish and she could at least have called the family and told them what the assignments were and they could write them down. The worst part was the reading journal; he was not getting practice reading books and talking about them because his parents could not fill out the sheet. I wish we had books in our classroom that were in Spanish because he could have taken those books home and his parents could have had conversations in Spanish about what happened and take their notes in Spanish. R. would have still be learning to read and practicing reading techniques, but it would have been in his home language and a language his parents understood.*

Another case study documented a student teacher who was interested in tying personal family stories and language into new learning contexts which were multilingual for many children. She had strong personal convictions about giving children opportunities to connect with others from different backgrounds. This student teacher also worked with kindergarten children.

LISTENING

She began by explaining to the children that in her family four languages are spoken at different times. Then she read *I Love Saturdays y Domingos* by Alma Flor Ada (2002)—a story about how a child has one set of grandparents who speaks Spanish and one set who speaks English. The child describes her visits to both families and what they do and what they say, in both Spanish and English.

DIALOGUE

After the story, the student teacher asked, "What did you learn about the girl's family? What were some differences about the different grandparents? what ways were the two grandparent families the same and different? How did they feel about the girl? The children noticed the different languages, the different ways of enjoying time together, and the different foods of each family. And they noticed that both families loved and were loved by the girl.

Then the class had a group discussion about all the different languages which are used in their own families and communities. The teacher extended the discussion in terms of sociolinguistics by asking, "How do you know which language to speak with which person?"

ACTION

A variety of "action opportunities" were available at the classroom centers:

1. At one center children could choose pictures to make a "family collage" to represent their family and write a short story in their home language, English, or both, about the family depicted in the collage.
2. At another center, there were recipe books from around the world and materials for children to "write" recipes of dishes their family likes to eat. There were also math manipulatives related to measurement for exploration at the same center.
3. There were CDs and tapes with music from around the world at the music center.
4. There was a variety of heavy card paper for children to write letters or invitations (in different languages) to family members.

For action outside the classroom:

1. She and the children went on a neighborhood walk and looked for different examples of print written in different languages. They stopped along the way and talked and showed each other bits of the script they saw. The children all had clipboards so that they could draw or write some details about where the script was found, such as if it was a store, what was sold there, or if it was a place of worship, how did they know?
2. She sent a letter home to families with the children, asking permission for the children to bring one artifact (i.e., a cooking utensil, a photo, etc.) from the family to share the story of this artifact and the family memory with the class.

After this brief experience and several others from her field work, she wrote:

In my experience in the classroom I have witnessed that children respond beautifully to learning about their classmates' cultures, values and languages. Singing in different languages or reading books about different cultures is thrilling for children. Children who are exposed to different cultures, values, and languages learn to respect one another and to appreciate their own cultures as well. I feel that children who are involved in a culturally supportive environment where they are encouraged to share their ideas become more confident about their own identity. When children develop their own sense of self they are more apt to respect others' differences. I saw children trying to teach each other their home languages as they moved through the activities. I saw children playing with and interacting with children whom they previously had no voluntary contact with. I plan to fully implement a curriculum that encourages all of the children to share and learn from each other's cultures and languages.

Another case documented a student teacher who wanted first graders to connect their own personal histories to a study of famous people from a historical, artistic and human rights standpoint, while focusing on all aspects of balanced literacy. The lesson began with the storybook Diego Rivera by Jeanette Winter (1991).

LISTENING

The student teacher asked the children to think again about something they really like to do and do well. She asked them to think about how they learned to do it? Then she read the book *Diego*.

DIALOGUE

The class discussed the activities that Diego did, how he practiced his talent, and how he expressed himself through art. The student teacher then asked children in what ways they preferred to express themselves.

Then the student teacher asked if the children noticed that the artist "painted what he saw?" They reviewed and discussed parts of the storybook that showed this. She asked, "Do you have any thoughts about why this artist felt he must paint these scenes?"

ACTION

The student teacher and the children created a Diego Bulletin Board, on which the children constantly contributed ideas (mirroring the chalkboard walls in the story) about what they had discussed and thought. During a Writing Workshop, the children wrote about what they had drawn.

They had a poetry writing activity, "Where am I from?/Where's my family from?" which involved the children in writing list poems based upon their own lives. There were encyclopedias, magazines, and websites provided so that the children could investigate art history and history books to learn about the context in which Diego Rivera lived and worked.

Two of the class' research questions based upon the children's questions as the lessons developed were: Why was Diego's hero Zapata? Why are Diego's murals found in various national buildings in Mexico City considered to be national treasures? The student teacher wrote:

Often it was in the context of the daily lessons that most of the children's "a-ha" moments happened relating to critical literacy. For example, when the children were learning about Diego Rivera the first graders began what became a three-day on-going discussion about which "art" or which type of "craft" was important and why and to whom. In the many discussions that ensued during the lessons about Diego Rivera, the children became fascinated by the phrase "he painted what he saw" and the fact that that meant beauty as well as suffering. A small group of children asked the teachers to bring books of artwork that depicted people fighting as in the demonstrations and riots that Diego Rivera painted.

So, what do we learn from children's and teachers' stories?

In many ways it is so simple. We learn that there are common threads which connect all learners across their context specificity. It is these threads which help teachers and those learning to be teachers connect with children and families from diverse cultures and learn about their differences. It is also through the variety of knowledge sources and personal histories that we learn from each other. Critical literacy curriculum activities provide many sources for addressing knowledge in all subject areas. In addition, most educators acknowledge that content knowledge alone does constitute an "education." Critical theorists agree that education has everything to do with citizenship. Making students aware that their cognitive life is not separate from social history has been the work of educators and artists. The beginning teachers discussed here are on their way to learning from students' stories.

CHAPTER SIXTEEN

Immigrants in Our Own Land

IRENE V. GARZA

Walking out the 5th graders to their buses, I overheard Julian sadly saying to anther students, "Nine more days of school, yea." The other students responded, "Why?" and Julian in a low voice replied, "I have to attend summer school, but quiero ir a Mexico." Hearing the student's conversation, I couldn't resist as Julian sounded so sad and so I told him, "Julian you have to attend summer school, Mexico can wait." Instantaneously, I saw Julian's eyes fill with tears. Rushing to comfort Julian, while also feeling an awful knot in my stomach, I asked, "Julian, what's wrong?" Julian sadly replied, "I want to go to Mexico to see my mother." I asked, "Is your mother in Mexico?" With tears in his eyes, Julian told me, "My mother was deported to Mexico three years ago by immigration and I want to go see her." There are no words to describe the pain and empathy I felt for Julian at that moment so I just blurted out, "Julian forget about summer school, you go and see your mother." I gave him a bit hug and just stood and watched as he got on his bus.

Immigration had been a staple of the United States since the Europeans themselves came and "occupied" the land that was already inhabited by other people and will continue, as this is a land made up of immigrants. Illegal immigration is out of control, the influx of Latino immigrants is huge, immigrants are taking jobs, and children of illegal immigrants are not citizens are a few of the reasons opponents of immigration cite. A few of the reasons for immigration are: that immigrants do the jobs Americans do not want to do, that immigrants have the right to get papers and citizenship, and that immigrants want a chance at a better life. Immigration has and will be an issue of controversy in this country for a very long time.

We can trace illegal immigration back to the British, as they were the first unwanted foreigners who came and encroached in large numbers on the lands of the Powhatan Indians on May 14, 1607. The unwanted English came and a lot of tension was created, as the English couldn't speak the Powhatan language, they looked and spoke differently. The English also stole the Powhatan lands. The point being that tensions associated with immigration hasn't changed much in the last 400 years. There exists so much tension due to newcomers looking and talking differently than most of us.

Presently, Hispanics are at the center of the immigration issue. Hispanics are seen as different as they are the first to pour into the American public square bearing Mexican flags and demanding instant citizenship without any penalty for having broken American laws. Mexicans have been on these lands way before the United States birth. As many Mexican say we didn't cross the river, the river crossed us.

Due to Mexico's vast land holdings, the government did not keep very close connections with the Mexicanos on the northern lands, and Anglos were able to migrate and settle easily. After the United States defeated Mexico and Santa Anna sold part of Mexico to the United States, life for the Mexicanos changed. Even though the Treaty of Hidalgo guaranteed protection of land and culture for the Mexican people, the U.S. amendments changed things for the Mexican people living in the land that now belonged to the United States.

Mexicans have had to endure 150 years of exclusion in the United States since the Treaty of Hidalgo in 1848. Since that time, Hispanic Americans have never been legally protected or given the same equal opportunities or consideration that the Constitution of the United States guarantees to every American. To this day, Latinos many times feel less like American citizens and more like recent immigrants or life-long foreigners in a country in which a great portion of the land used to belong to our Mexican ancestry and which once was our country (Portales, 2000).

Immigration, whether here illegally or here when this land belonged to Mexico still effects all Mexicans, Mexican Americans, Chicanos, etc., as we are a group that was here before and continues to challenge the United States' melting pot view. As a community we have close proximity to our ancestry (Mexican-aspect of ourselves), retain our native language, continue and share many of the customs of our Mexican heritage. Hispanics have been a fear for the United States since the first two decades of the 20th century. The fear began gaining strength because of our rate of immigration and our ability to assimilate into traditional American cultural boundaries associated with middle class (Blanton, 2004). Americans were fearful of the New Mexican immigrant. Today, that fears continues as the influx of Latino immigrants continues as well as the fear of the awakening of the sleeping giant. With Latinos, it is not only an issue with immigration, but with the Latino's demand to bringing ourselves to the public square demanding instant citizenship.

Opponents of immigration say that too many illegal immigrants are taxing the U.S. economy, taking jobs, and that children of illegal immigrants are not citizens. Yet, because of the low birth rate in the United State, which results in low numbers of people of age to work, the United States has a need that immigrants can fill.

In the past and presently today the United Stats has depended on cheap immigrant labor and whether here legally or not, the Mexican laborer has been filling a niche the United States has needed. The first major wave of Mexican workers into the United States began in the early twentieth century after the decline of cheap Asian labor and limitation of Japanese immigration (Pettus, 2007). When the United States entered World War I the need for Mexican labor increased tremendously due to the decrease of cheap immigrant labor from other countries, and due to Mexico's close proximity to the United States. Mexico became a "convenient source of cheap immigrant labor," (Gutierrez, 1997). The United States sought an agreement with the Mexican government to export Mexican laborers as farm workers, which allowed U.S. workers to fight overseas (Pettus, 2007). These workers would ensure the continued food supply during the war years. Thus was born the bracero.

THE BRACERO

With the full knowledge and consent of the Mexican government, this movement of Mexican laborers began with full knowledge of no entitlement to permanent immigration for the bracero or Mexican national, as they were also known (Eldridge, 1957).

> Not until 1942, as the United States entered World War II, were Mexican immigrants allowed to reenter in large numbers. To stem labor shortages in industries that were deemed essential to the war effort, Congress authorized Public Law 45, which became widely known as the bracero program. Though this legislation was initially deemed a temporary emergency war measure, it was repeatedly extended in various forms and slightly different names until 1964. (Gutierrez, 1997)

Started in 1942, as a wartime emergency measure, (Eldridge, 1957) the bracero program was enacted as Public Law 78. "Approximately 4.6 million braceros entered the United States between 1942 and 1964, a statistic considered accurate by most American and Mexican authorities" (Gutierrez, 1997). The braceros worked in many states: Far Western states, some spots of the prairie states, Middle West as far north as Michigan, the South and along the Mexican border. "In the early 1960s with the advent of the civil-rights movement, public opinion began to view the Bracero system as exploitative and detrimental to the socioeconomic condition of Mexican Americans" (Pettus, 2007).

Although the U.S. government sought Mexico's agreement to relieve its labor shortage due to shortage of labor workers due to the United States' involvement in the war overseas, braceros faced many problems before and after becoming braceros.

The bracero faced many problems before he even arrived in the United States. He entered on this journey with the knowledge that he could be rejected. The bracero usually had to borrow money to begin the process, which included paying his expenses to reach the recruiting station. Usually the first step involved going to the presidente municipal (mayor) and to ask either for a certificado o un permiso (certificate or a permission). The Mexican national had to be of good moral standing, be unemployed and not owning any land given to him by the government. Many times braceros had to pay between300 and 350 pesos; (at that time, a peso was worth approximately eight American cents and a campesino averaged between seven and ten pesos a day) a bracero would usually pay the mordida. Once that was completed, he also had to prove he had completed his compulsory military service (Eldridge, 1957).

He faced a long wait while getting all his documentation ready in Mexico and still faced a long wait before he got to the U.S. pipeline that would get him to the American farmer who would hire him. Although many campesinos joined the ranks of becoming braceros, many did not follow the legal process of getting permisos. This group came as libres (free literally free men) and if they were patient they normally got into the pipeline.

Once in the pipeline, braceros, whether in the pipeline as Mexican nationals or libres still faced many problems. A problem many faced was of being assigned to a short contract, which would not even cover their invested expense. Other problems facing the braceros were "unsanitary living conditions, payment failures, peonage contracts, overt racism," (Gutierrez, 1997) being cheated out of wages earned by farmers who manipulated the hours worked and got away without having to pay the Mexican nationals a decent wage (Eldridge, 1957). Even though braceros faced many problems there were some experiences for the braceros that were not always negative. According to my grandfather's recollection, the braceros would come and work near his hometown at the surrounding ranches and they were treated decently. My grandfather remembered that even Border Patrol agents would at times give the braceros a ride to their destinations around the Encinal (La Salle county, TX.) area. Although, braceros faced problems they did it to try to improve their family's standard of living.

Becoming a bracero was not an easy task for campesinos to undertake, but they ventured into the unknown to work in the United States to be able to give their families a little more financial support, "of raising his family's standard of living above that of the barest subsistence" (Eldridge). "I came to America," said a campesino, "because my family and I are very poor" (Eldridge, 1957). "Being landless and unable to produce or purchase the basic necessities of life," (Gutierrez, 1997) these men were forced to seek work opportunities away from their families.

Although braceros faced many obstacles, there were obvious economic benefits for Mexico's population. Many braceros saved money and upon returning to Mexico built homes for their families, or invested in small plots of lands and purchased animals. Others sent money to Mexico, "One bracero camp of 1700 men in Fullerton, California, sent $316,000 home during three months in 1956" (Eldridge, 1957). The bracero program also lowered the unemployment rate and raised wages, something that the Mexican government was not able to do. Even though the bracero program ended in 1964, many immigrants still follow the path to the United States in hopes of raising their family's standard of living.

Whether here legally or illegally many Mexican labor workers remain among the lowest paid workers in the country, many times without job security or benefits (Heinicke & Grove, 2005).

> The act of moving from one nation to another, often with few financial resources, requires an exceptional degree of drive, courage, and resourcefulness. There's something special about a person who's willing to put up with everything you have to put up with to be an immigrant. (Pettus, 2007)

Faced with so many obstacles, the Mexican labor worker continues the journey north into the United States in order to one day improve their family's standard of living. Due to Mexican immigrants' immigration to the United States, the question of appropriate policy immigrants continues as a recurrent concern for various interest groups in the United States (Gutierrez, 1997). The immigration of Mexicans has been seen as both a problem and an asset. As a problem Mexican immigration has been viewed as threatening the racial, hygienic, and economic basis of life in the United States. As an asset Mexican immigration contributes to U.S. prosperity by performing tasks at wages that citizen workers will not accept, and by contributing to the tax fund of the United States while being excluded from reaping their benefits (Gutierrez, 1997). Advocates for Mexican immigration favor less government regulations and open doors. Those against Mexican immigration demand severe Mexican immigration restrictions. While the continual disagreements in relation to Mexican immigration continue between proponents and opponents Mexican immigrants will continue living between two distinct worlds. Immigration affects all people of Mexican heritage, and there have been times in U.S. history when we have faced deportation just because of our race.

In the 1930s massive repatriation campaigns were conducted in many areas of the United States, especially in areas concentrated with people of Mexican descent. According to reports at the state and federal levels, the people deported were all Mexicans. "The reality was that many Americans of Mexican descent were deported or emigrated back to Mexico under duress" (Gutierrez, 1997). My grandparents lived in the border city of Laredo, Texas and witnessed the deportation of Mexican Americans just because of their race.

According to my grandparents, in the 1930s, many Mexicans were deported to Mexico. My grandmother vividly recalls seeing the Border Patrol around her neighborhood in Laredo, Texas rounding up Mexicans. She vividly remembers some Mexican Americans who lived in her neighborhood who were deported. The United States has used Mexican labor to fit its needs, while at the same time denying Mexicans of their rightful citizenship when it has wanted to just because a person is of Mexican descent.

Immigration is an issue that has affected the lives of the whole Mexican community. We continue to live as we have for over five hundred years as a race caught between two countries and languages and not being accepted by either Mexico or the United States. Presently, Democrats want to introduce a bill that would give most illegal immigrants a path to immigration. Points of contention of the bill are whether temporary workers will have a chance for citizenship, whether certain family-based immigration categories will be eliminated, and whether immigrants will have to go back their home countries before returning back.

Knowing the legacy of the Anglos toward the whole Mexican community after the Treaty of Hidalgo in 1848, can we really trust the government to do right by the Mexican American people? We have to count on the American people to decide whether honest, hard-working people should be treated like criminals or whether to keep families together.

Mexicans have two things guaranteed for them: the 12 million-plus illegal immigrants cannot all be deported. Hispanics can change this country significantly through its culture and language. A stronger and more united coalition needs to be built to gain legal status and rights for immigrants and better employment opportunities and better wages for all labor workers who are still "unprepared for higher paying occupations" (Heinicke & Grove, 2005).

The Hispanic community needs to continue to rally in order for our needs and opinions to become known. We need to awaken the sleeping giant to gain full participation in American society we face many obstacles, yet we have been here way before the Europeans came and "occupied" our land and we are taking charge of our destiny, as this has always been our home. Whether we identify as Mexicans, Mexican American, Latinos, Hispanics, Chicanos, etc. we must unite and rally as a united village to eventually attain our rightful place in our own land.

CHAPTER SEVENTEEN

Teachers Rethinking Their Pedagogical Attitudes in the Bicultural/Bilingual Classroom

HAROOM KHAREM & GENEVIEVE COLLURA

The issue of what qualifies as knowledge in teaching—as well as whose knowledge matters—affects teachers' lives and constitutes many of the most pervasive, frustrating philosophy/reality conflicts.

> JOLONGO & ISENBERG (1995, P. 14)

I desire mercy, not sacrifice

> (MATTHEW 9:12) NEW INTERNATIONAL VERSION.

INTRODUCTION

Reform in bicultural/bilingual education is a necessity in the United States. Students in this country are taught by a particular standard that works to marginalize a large number of students. These marginalized "others" are taught to lose their identity and learn to become part of a group without a voice. We must, as educators, teach our students how to critically navigate and articulate their bicultural/bilingual culture, how to communicate their own identities to prevent a loss of culture, language, and history (Bohn & Sleeter 2001; Foucault, 1984, p. 180).

Although the state of New York's multicultural standard for social studies clearly states to include multiculturalism or culturally relevant pedagogy, literacy and mathematics test prep takes precedence. The fact is, the population of bilingual/bicultural children is increasing each year, and teachers must accommodate their curricula to fit the needs of those who are losing their identities without conceptualizing what these students are missing to be successful in the classroom.

In this chapter we argue that the most pressing challenges for teachers are the presence of a large population of bicultural/bilingual students and a culture war that disparages students whose culture is not Anglo Protestant, who speak another language, and whose skin is non-white. We also argue that teachers need to understand the political, historical ramifications of promoting Anglo Protestantism as superior. Educators must comprehend that the media has enormous impact on teachers and their pedagogy. Teachers in turn teach a banking curriculum where learners are thought to be like docile empty vessels who can be assimilated into the Anglo Protestant culture and language. Bicultural/bilingual students are forced to erase their culture and rely on the Anglo Protestant perspective embedded in the present social order and belief systems. We hope to make obvious the ideological implications.

Foucault's "Docile Bodies" is descriptive of what can happen to a child without the presence of critical multicultural education in the classroom. Foucault writes, "a body that is docile...may be subjected, used, transformed, and improved (p. 180)." If we teach our children to be docile by excluding critical multiculturalism in the classroom, we are in danger of seeing parallels of machines that can be "improved" to fit into our school systems. Paulo Freire (1985) refers to this docile pedagogy as "domestication," where knowledge is deposited into passive students through manipulation (p. 102). Stripping our students of their culture, their right to question, and deliberately excluding critical thinking in the classroom can domesticate and result in a docile individual.

This kind of pedagogy must be questioned. Teachers must let go of the meticulous control over the nature of our children's minds, to reverse the possibility of their becoming both predictable and malleable to the American school system. However, teachers have to first understand these complex issues in order to make an effort to prevent domestication from happening. Teachers are given charge of other people's children and what happens in the early years of that charge will leave an impression upon the child that will follow them for the rest of their lives.

IDEOLOGICAL LIES MAINTAINED AS TRUTHS

We thought to share in this essay a conversation I (Professor Kharem) witnessed between two elementary school teachers conversing about a Muslim parent who did not want her child to participate in the Thanksgiving activities in the classroom. The teachers had their students making various Thanksgiving items centered around a lesson on the traditional story of the Pilgrims and the Native indigenous people sitting down, eating and giving thanks to the Christian God for the bountiful harvest He supposedly bestowed upon them. One of the teachers commented that if people are going to immigrate to America then they should learn to participate in our culture and customs or leave.

As I proceeded to leave the teacher's lounge to observe a lesson of one of the teacher candidates in the school, I asked both teachers: "Should we stop celebrating Kwanza because some Whites want us to conform to European Christian cultural norms? Should we stop giving Jews allowances from school and work to celebrate Rosh Hashanah, Yom Kippur and other holidays they observe in New York City? Do we force people to leave the U.S. who do not practice Anglo Christian customs?"

I walked away thinking about the claim that teachers are to be politically and culturally neutral. I also contemplated upon their lack of knowledge of the real facts about Thanksgiving and its fabricated origin. Millions of people celebrate an "embarrassing" myth that originally had nothing to do with the Pilgrims or the Native indigenous people until the late 1800s when both (the Pilgrims and the Native indigenous people) were inserted into a day of prayer started by President Abraham Lincoln in 1863 to drum up patriotic support during the Civil War (Loewen, 2007, p. 90).

I was agitated by the teachers' colonized mind and their apathetic attitude concerning their responsibility as teachers to research on whether the story of Thanksgiving really happened the way they teach it to children. They took it for granted (as do thousands of teachers) that the traditional Thanksgiving story is factual truth and teach it to children every year. We assume students do not see through the indoctrination or mythical factoids taught to them, while at the same time disrespecting Native American indigenous people whose story is different from the mainstream Anglo-Protestant story. We want to keep celebrating Thanksgiving and seek ways to justify the dinner by coming up with new ideas in order not to be embarrassed and ashamed that we celebrate a holiday that gives thanks for the genocide of indigenous people (Rains, 2003).

The Puritan governor of Massachusetts, John Winthrop, praised his Christian God of love for destroying the indigenous population with diseases by calling it "miraculous" (Jennings, 1975; Simpson, 1980). Teachers teach the Thanksgiving story as gospel truth and any student who might question its validity may find him or herself in trouble. Susan Shown Harjo (1998) describes the Native indigenous people's perspective about us celebrating a lie and the beginning of their demise and destruction. Harjo said it eloquently in her essay "We Have No Reason to Celebrate an Invasion" that "teachers need to respect the truth" and not teach lies to children in the name of patriotism (p. 13). Instead, a pedagogy of stupidification is promoted in which teachers imbue students with untruths and then wonder why education has problems. Sooner or later the fabrications we teach students will come to light and the respect educators expect from students will become disingenuous (Macedo, 2006).

Harjo rightfully questions our commitment as educators to respect the craft of teaching, to research what we teach, and reassess our commitment to the diverse learners sitting in our classrooms. In addition, she questions teachers' commitment to respect the various cultural backgrounds of their students who are marginalized, oppressed, and stamped as the "other."

The idea of teachers encouraging children to draw and cut out turkeys, pumpkins, and other items to hang up in the classroom is a sham and a lie. Michael Dorris (1998) says we "burden our children with [our] own unexamined mental junk" by imbuing them with lessons of the Pilgrims inviting the Native indigenous people to a feast "the Pilgrims...literally (had) never seen" themselves (p. 76). The subtle and sometimes outright Americanization of immigrants or students whose beliefs and cultural systems are different can be labeled totalitarian.

A PEDAGOGY THAT PROMOTES FAILURE

This is not the only occurrence that demonstrates the injustices imbedded in the way we teach and treat children. The public school system is not made to fit the needs of bilingual/bicultural children. The New York City Department of Education's Regulation of the Chancellor regarding promotional status is just one example of the institutional injustice within schools. According to this document, "English Language Learners (ELL) with disabilities receiving special education services that have not been enrolled in an English Language School System (ELSS) for less than two years are not held to promotional standards (New York City Department of Education Standards English Language Learners)." This means that ELL students are moved ahead to the next grade, even if they do not understand the material or the "English" language in which it is taught for the two years. Teachers usually pass this dilemma off as a "language" or "culture" adjustment, as they deem it necessary.

These students are stripped of their language and unable to communicate their culture, and then asked to take standardized tests beginning in the third grade. If a student arrives in this country in the first grade and is pushed ahead for two years without understanding some of the content due to translation needs, how is the child supposed to understand and take a standardized test? Are we deliberately setting these children up to fail? This is where bicultural/bilingual children are left behind, not understanding the material or the reason why they cannot understand it. Students are left discouraged, frustrated and then marginalized to the outskirts of society to languish in poverty; they are employed in low income jobs or see crime as the only option.

Predictably enough, instead of focusing on the school system and how our children are taught, culture and language differences are always to blame. We talked about different occasions where we expressed concerns to some teachers whose attitudes reflect that it is not their problem if students do not "understand English." They feel it is not "their problem" or are not sensitive to the linguistic insecurities of a child and pass her/him onto the next grade—the teachers thus label the child as insubordinate because the child resists letting go of their native home language. Consequently, the language problem is left for future teachers to try and keep the students on their current grade level while at the same time correct what was not accomplished in the lower grades. This intensifies the stress upon the bicultural/bilingual student and increases the chances of failure. Thus, schools push young children to resist classroom instruction as they cling to what little self-respect they have for their native language and culture. The passive students are imbued to devalue their own home language for standard Anglo-Protestant middle-class discourse, which only exacerbates their own linguistic insecurities, while others develop resistance to protect their native culture. It compels us to ask who the real perpetuators of violence in schools are. Donaldo Macedo and Lilia Bartolomé (1999) contend teachers' uncaring attitudes leave psychological scars and place the failure solely upon bicultural/bilingual students. They add that teachers would rather blame students than look at their own pedagogical failure (p. 70).

Nonetheless, is this not a clear indication that teachers need to work harder to embrace the culture of their children, to give them as much attention as possible before they are pushed ahead without knowing what is going on from grade to grade? Should we not wonder about what will happen to these students once they are pushed along until they have to pass a standardized test? Is it not the responsibility of the teachers to make sure that these students are getting the best instruction possible in the classroom with such regulations in place? Mary Hatwood Futrell and Elaine P. Witty (1997) argue that the future of marginalized bicultural/bilingual children rests in the reform of current guidelines that relate not only to the standards but also to the reform of discriminatory policies set in place by the dominant culture. Futrell and Witty favor preparation and professional development programs that will produce teachers who are well trained in culturally relevant pedagogy and instruction, thus providing avenues for all students to meet high standards.

Inevitably, along with these language differences and difficulty in translation from one's native language to English are the accompanying stigmas and stereotypes. Lois Weiner disputes what some of the past research suggests as the "culture" of the students and their families being deficit and responsible for their academic failure.

This can be due to the differences in cultural practices where students come from, or it could be that the students are not translating the English language in their minds fast enough to understand what is being taught. It is then easy to blame others for failure, when teachers do not reflect on what is really happening (Weiner, 1999).

The most dangerous effect is students believing that they are to blame for not understanding the material and teachers not recognizing that the curriculum and methodology used in instruction must change to accommodate the bicultural/bilingual students. Self-confirming stereotypes are generalizations about a class of people that are considered to be true "with reason," but cannot really be determined to be true or false based on the individuals. It is important that teachers do not instill these beliefs in the children they serve. If students begin to fail because of the situation they are exposed to, students must also be able to succeed when exposed to a classroom that nurtures and understands their background (Loury, 2002).

A PEDAGOGY THAT DEVALUES THE "OTHER"

While bicultural/bilingual children are in the process of being Americanized, they are also taught to devalue their own language and culture, and thus blamed for failing to understand what is going on in the classroom. They are being subtly taught through classroom instruction and textbooks that U.S. expansion was benign, promoted civilization, ordained by God and use the Bible to support their claim of Manifest Destiny. The cultural Americanization of people is still little understood as millions of children have been and are continually instilled with American/Anglo-Protestant stories of its past as if they are all true. Americanization becomes the pedagogical tool to promote a color-blind society where the goal is to imbue students with the idea that race and ethnicity have no bearing upon the decisions made that may affect their lives. Under the umbrella of a color-blind ideology some teachers claim they see no color and therefore race is erased from the classroom as they try to pretend all the kids are White (Merk, 1963; Paley, 1989; Stephanson, 1995; Zinn, 2003).

Schools claim to support critical thinking but actually indoctrinate children not to think critically and force a blind allegiance to those who have a vested interest in the present system. While the United States is one of the most powerful and wealthiest nations on earth, its education system produces a high number of dysfunctionally illiterate readers who are deliberately miseducated. Few understand that a curriculum of stupidification is in the ideological interest of the dominant culture to maintain its power and privileged position (Chomsky, 2000; Macedo, 2006).

Conservative scholars like E. D. Hirsch, Allan Bloom, William Bennett, Diane

Ravitch, John Silber alongside others have attacked diverse cultural epistemologies that question traditional Western cultural hegemonic knowledge. Western cultural knowledge historically demonized and set out to colonize other ethnic and racial groups in the name of civilization. Europe and the United States colonized various regions around the world, forcing indigenous peoples to attend colonial schools, adopt the colonial languages, and produce indigenous leaders to control the discontented masses. For instance, U.S. multinational corporations consistently encourage the removal of the indigenous population, take control of large tracts of land that displaces the farmers and others into crowded urban centers, and put in place government leaders who will follow U.S. policies that are detrimental to their own citizens. When the people have resisted and taken up arms to regain their land, the United States historically sent in the Marines to put down any civil discontentment (Altbach & Kelly 1978; Constantino, 1978; Fanon , 2004).

The U.S. media disparages Latinos who have sought to escape their war-torn and poverty-stricken countries influenced by U.S. foreign policies of the recent Reagan-Bush era. After the second Gulf War, the United States is presently trying to Westernize the Islamic countries with Western culture and consumerism under the guise of democracy. At the same time we racialize and label these same people as "rag heads," "towel heads," "sand niggers," and those who disagree with U.S. policy are called either terrorists or insurgents in their own countries. For the moment the racist pedagogy is slanted towards those of Arab or Middle Eastern descent. The irony of all this is that some African Americans have joined in with the use of derogatory racial language against the Islamic religion and culture. American schools have colonized the minds of Black people and some of us have forgotten that at one time we (Blacks and other non-whites) were called derogatory names. We have forgotten that some Whites were telling us (and some still do) to 'go back to Africa' and that Africa never had any civilized history worth studying (Chomsky, 1979; 1999; Elliot, 2006).

Students are depoliticized, taught to support and rally behind an ideology that is not only destructive but also colonial and imperialistic under the guise of democracy and globalization. We have bastardized the African proverb "It takes a whole village to raise a child" to mean that we are a global village, the Third World must share its natural resources with the West. Yet, the United States still uses imperialistic adventures to control the world's resources under the disguise of globalization. The Filipino intellectual Renato Constantino (1978) said the mental colonization of the Filipino people "manifested itself most harmfully in the myths that were deeply ingrained in the Filipino consciousness (p. 78)." Constantino emphasized that Americans saw the Filipino people as little children in need of guidance and parenting in the ways of democracy. He argued that the imposition of the English language upon Filipino schools improved literacy "but this literacy was also a form of illiteracy. Because of the imposition of a foreign language, the children, most of whom reached only grade school, were barely able to read and write (p. 79). This "functional illiteracy" produced ambivalent minds, allowed government, administrative, and economic positions to the miseducated upper classes that had a "distorted view" of the needs of the people, and the colonized followed the interests of the colonizer.

As Blacks have struggled and opened the floodgates for other ethnic and racial groups to participate in and enjoy full citizenship in the United States, we cannot forget that this nation is presently engaged in a form of racial and religious oppression that has turned the historical clock back to the Crusades. Also let us critically examine why the story of the Pilgrims and Native indigenous people eating a Thanksgiving dinner was created. We need to understand that there was never a dinner; in fact the Pilgrims were too busy thanking their God for killing off the indigenous people to satisfy their own selfish schemes.

Teacher education is mostly concerned with preparing potential teachers with methods and classroom management, instead of with the racial and cultural knowledge to stand in front of the various ethnic and racial groups that fill up their classrooms (Fine, et al., 1997; Ladson-Billings, 1997 & 1999). The question is not whether schools of education have a multicultural course for teacher candidates and practicing teachers; the question is whether schools of education are immersed in culturally relevant pedagogy and instruction that will prepare teacher candidates to critically look at and understand the diverse bicultural/bilingual student population that is changing the American landscape. Do teachers and teacher candidates have a working knowledge of the diverse cultures of the numerous students in their classrooms? Also, do teachers and teacher candidates understand the effect of an Anglo-Protestant education system on the learning styles of children from other ethnic, racial, and religious cultural norms? We need to ask whether college schools of education are preparing culturally relevant teachers not just in theory but in practice (Hale-Benson, 1982; Irvine, 1997; Ladson-Billings, 1999, 2001, & 2003; McCarthy & Crichlow, 1993).

As we address multiculturalism in the classroom, we do not want to continue to teach history and culture through the eyes of important or powerful people nor continue to marginalize the poor, underprivileged, and disenfranchised off to the side as the "other." A critical multicultural pedagogy is not inviting the parents of students for a pot-luck extravaganza or a day of ethnic costumes. Just as Euro-American students are taught to value and be proud of their history and cultural heritage, we should be teaching in a way that allows all students to own their history, culture, language, and ideas. Bill Bigelow and associates (2001) discuss that "good teaching begins with a respect for children, their innate curiosity and their capacity to learn." In other words, good teaching is student centered; the keystone of the curricula rests upon the needs, experiences, and lives of the children in the classroom. This will allow students to build confidence and be proud of who they are and where they come from (Harding, 1990; Rains, 2003; Zinn & Macedo, 2005).

SETTING THE CAPTIVES FREE

Foucault (1984) speaks of Panopticism, or the concept of an all-seeing eye constantly watching to correct and normalize against "agitations, revolts, spontaneous organizations, (or) coalitions (p. 204)." This concept is based on a building of Jeremy Bentham's. This building allowed officers to stand from a center tower and watch those incarcerated, while those in the prison were unable to see their observers from the buildings where they were held captive (p. 206–213). We do not want our students to be trained to feel as though a teacher who acts as the all-seeing eye watches students carefully to correct them if they are not speaking English or come from another country. Instead we must instill a sense of pride in our students that will help them grow individually and collaboratively in the classroom. Many students must meet standards that are very demanding for children who must learn how to first speak English, and then master reading, comprehending, and practicing strategies in every subject independently.

When the odds are against our children, emotional support is important in the classroom. Daniel Goleman explains that "hazards await those who, in growing to maturity, fail to master the emotional realm—how deficiencies in emotional intelligence heighten a spectrum of risks, from depression to a life of violence to eating disorders and drug abuse." The emotional realm must be understood and mastered by the teacher to help students succeed. As a teacher, I (Master Teacher Genevieve Collura) strive to work toward the teachings of Goleman in my classroom, in order to provide the support children from different backgrounds need to succeed in the American school system (Goleman, 1995).

Before teaching students who were learning English there were many concerns. As a classroom teacher, I want to make sure students understand that it is safe to make mistakes in the classroom. Students should feel comfortable speaking in their own language and in English. If students have a safe haven in the classroom, they will feel comfortable and motivated to learn English, but also understand that they do not need to lose their identities or languages to be successful in the classroom. I want students to be empowered through their language and cultures, but I also envisioned more allies in the public school community who would feel the same way about multicultural education.

I distinctly remember one of my first professional development sessions in my school, which focused on teaching ELL. The woman who was training us that day was extremely passionate about students of non-English speaking backgrounds all having a chance to succeed in an educational setting, while keeping their identity. She explained to the staff that many ELL students who learn English as a second language have trouble adjusting to new school systems. She added that we all had to be very conscious of the variety of cultures and languages in our classrooms. She spoke about how it is harder for some of the children who do not speak English as their first languages if they are exposed to teachers who tell them that they may not speak their own language in the classroom. A woman raised her hand and asked the question: "Well, why should we let them speak their own languages in the classroom? Doesn't that defeat the purpose of teaching English?" In response to this question, she asked us how we, as teachers, would feel if someone told us that we were not allowed to speak English in the room we were in. It would be a mixture of cultures lingering in seats, hoping that someone would know another common language in which we could all communicate.

Allowing children who are still learning English to communicate with others in the classroom of their own ethnicity allows them to feel safe, and helps them to understand things taught to a greater extent. This is especially true if the students communicating are on different levels of understanding English, since students who have more knowledge of English can help students translate who may be having difficulties. I have tried this in my own classroom and students gain social skills and comprehend more of the material taught.

As Goleman states,

"it is in a cauldron of close friendships and the tumult of play that children refine the social and emotional skills that they will bring to relationships later in life. Children who are excluded from this realm of learning are, inevitably, disadvantaged." (Goleman, 1995)

Students need close relationships in the classroom with the teacher and peers in order for them to succeed to the best of their ability.

We also talked about trying to bridge the gap between school and home. Using translators to help teachers write notes home or asking for languages other than English in standard letters were some ideas that were discussed. As this conversation proceeded, however, the topic of conversation changed quickly.

An administrator in training raised her hand. She said, "I don't mean to cut this conversation short, but honestly, I can say that I know that some cultures and races just do not want to participate in this. I mean some of the students and their parents are just, well, lazy. I mean I just wanted to say that, and I know from experience, trust me, it is true." An ESL teacher sat off to the side during this statement and nodded, and then added, "Well, some are...this is very true...but, not Russians, Russians are good...very good."

These comments brought numerous thoughts to my mind. I wondered if I should say something. There I was, faced with blatant stereotypical racism, a vulgar comment from an educator who was training to be an administrator. I also was confronted with another woman who specifically worked with English Second Language learners. Should I challenge what they said, or maybe just let their comments go unchallenged because of their position or work relations?

I thought back to the concept of color-blindness. Howard Winant (1994) put it very eloquently in stating, "race is a relatively impermeable part of our identities.

U.S. society is so thoroughly racialized that to be without racial identity is to be in danger of having no identity (p. 16)." The notion of color-blindness extends to teachers and administrators who claim not to be a part of it or that they are fair to all children.

There we were, a group of teachers participating in a professional development session on something that really matters for the children we are teaching, and someone says that certain ethnic/racial groups are lazy and may not want to succeed. I raised my hand.

"How could you say that a person is lazy, based on their ethnicity, culture, or on language differences?" I asked. "Is it really fair to say that? Don't you think it is hard to adjust to another culture or language, if you are foreign to it?" With these words, I received no response, so I proceeded. I wanted to give them an example of how Americans are exposed to the same things when they are introduced to a culture and language that is foreign to them, so they could understand.

I gave an example of one of my good friends, a White male who is considered educated by American standards. He was a double major in computer science and English. When he graduated with his degree he decided to move to Madrid, Spain, and work there. He figured there would be a teaching opportunity or perhaps something he could do with computers when he arrived. He knew he might have a bit of trouble at first finding a job because of his poor Spanish speaking skills, but he decided to try his luck. Upon his arrival he stayed with a friend until he began learning more Spanish.

He walked dogs for a living to pass the time and to clear his mind and communicate with others as he learned the native language of Madrid. There he was, a man who had just graduated college, in the same spot as many students and parents who are from different parts of the globe, just trying to survive in a place that was different from where he was born. I explained that some people could have seen him as lazy because they could have assumed that he did not know the language and just was not trying to learn. Perhaps they may have also assumed that he was uneducated because he did not speak Spanish or have a "prestigious" job. However, this was not the case. The fact that he did not have a "prestigious" job nor fully understood Spanish did not make him a lazy or an uneducated man. He was far from that stereotype, as are the people who come to America from other countries.

After the session was over, the woman giving the professional development thanked me for participating for speaking up and responding to the racial stereotypes made in the session by some teachers and administrators. This whole discussion really made me reflect on teachers who worked with our bilingual/bicultural students, and I wondered whether they were able to actually teach and help students with these stereotypes embedded in their way of thought. Instead of feeling bad about this, however, I decided to make sure that in my classroom students would always feel prideful and confident that they could do their best, no matter where they came from. The sadness and shock I felt from the professional development session was turned into something beautiful and empowering that should be instilled in all classrooms. Applying the emotional supportive practices of Goleman and rejecting the intrusive nature of Foucault's description of panopticism allowed me as a professional to achieve my goals of teaching bilingual/bicultural children.

This experience demonstrates the fact that many schools of education do not allow or motivate teacher candidates to critically examine the intractable problems of education; there is no recognition that racism and poverty, compounded by inequitable opportunities, are connected to education policies (Kozol, 2005) Some teachers and teacher candidates have resorted to the concept of color-blindness in education, thereby rendering any discussion on race a meaningless rhetorical classroom exercise. Educators and teachers are encouraged to acknowledge differences but de-emphasize the importance of race and culture. Nor are teachers or teacher candidates allowed to discuss and examine how overt racial attitudes and behaviors (macroaggressions) and unconscious, subtle racist behaviors (microaggressions) are manifested in schools and society (Crenshaw, 1995; Lawrence, 1995; Solorzano, 1998). Schools defend their stance claiming that they are neutral and religion is not a part of their curriculum; however, just look at the various holidays such as Easter, Thanksgiving, and Christmas; yet elementary classrooms across the United States perform plays, draw and cut out the various icons that are associated with these holidays every year. Teacher education argues that teachers take a neutral position in the classroom, yet the very fact one decides to teach implies a political stance and a cultural point of view that will ultimately come through in the classroom. Education is a political act and will never be neutral or unbiased due to the nature of its dependence upon political and economic leaders (Freire, 1985).

The act of teachers refusing to address the struggles of their students against racism, power, and discrimination is a political act to not engage students in meaningful discussions that are connected to their lives. Thus, the teacher participates and aligns himself/herself with forces that claim race does not matter in a society that built its infrastructure on race and discrimination. (The appeal of color-blindness by many is that they believe race can be transcended, thus delegitimizing and devaluing the impact of race on non-whites.) Paulo Freire (1985) argues that education by its very nature is a political act and those who decide to become educators and teachers are making a political decision to imbue others with their ideas and belief systems (Allen, 1994; Gotanda, 1995; Kharem, 2006; Peller, 1995). Howard Zinn and Donaldo Macedo (2005) explain:

> "In all (these) instances of racial...mistreatment, it is important for students to understandthat the roots of such hostility are social, environmental, and situational and are not an inevitability of human nature. It is also important to show how these antagonisms so divide people from one another as to make it difficult for them to solve their common problems in united action." (p. 196)

Changes must take place in our minds in order for bicultural/bilingual children of America to succeed when the odds are against them, or we will remain a race of teachers and children who refuse to empower our children to think critically. We need to allow our students to unite as a community of multicultural learners in order for them to succeed in keeping their own identities, cultures, and languages in our American school system today.

Bibliography

Ada, Alma Flor (2004). *I Love Saturdays Y Domingos*. New York: Atheneum.

Alarcón, Francisco X. (2005). *From the Bellybutton of the Moon: And Other Summer Poems / Del Ombligo de la Luna: Y Otros Poemas de Verano*. San Francisco, CA: Children's Book Press.

Alarcón, F. X. (1997). *Laughing Tomatoes and Other Spring Poems / Jitomates risueños y otros poemas de primavera*. San Francisco: Children's Book Press.

Allen, Theodore W. (1994). *The Invention of the White Race: Racial Oppression and the Social Contract*. New York: Verso Press.

Allexsaht-Snider, Martha (1996). "Windows into Diverse Worlds: The Telling and Sharing of Teachers' Life Histories." *Education and Urban Society*. 29, 103–119.

Altbach, Philip G. & Kelly, Gail P. (1978). *Education and Colonialism*. New York: Longman.

Ani, Marimba (1994). *Yurugu: An African-Centered Critique of European Cultural Thought and Behavior*. Trenton, NJ: Africa World Press.

Anselmo, Angela & Rubal-Lopez, Alma (2005). *On Becoming Nuyoricans*. New York: Peter Lang.

Anzaldúa, Gloria (1999). *Borderlands/la Frontera: The New Mestiza*. (2nd ed.). San Francisco, CA: Aunt Lute Books.

Arce, Josephine (2004). "Latino Bilingual Teachers: The Struggle to Sustain an Emancipatory Pedagogy in Public Schools." *International Journal of Qualitative Studies in Education*. 17(2), 227–246.

Artz, Lee & Murphy, Bren Ortega (2000). *Cultural Hegemony in the United States*. Thousand Oaks, CA: Sage.

Ashcroft, B.; Griffiths, Gareth & Tiffin, Helen (1995). *The Post-Colonial Studies Reader*. New York: Routledge.

Asher, N. (2007). Made in the (multicultural) U.S.A.: Unpacking tensions of race, culture, gender, and sexuality in education. *Educational Researcher*, 36 (2), 65-73.

Ayers, William & Ford, Patricia (Eds.). (1996). *City Kids City Teachers: Reports from the Front Row*. New York: The New Press.

Bacon, David. (2005). "Beyond Braceros." *The Nation*. 281(December 8), 5–6.

Baker, Colin (2006). *Foundations of Bilingual Education and Bilingualism*. Tonawanda, NY: Multilingual Matters.

Bateson, Mary C. (1995). *Peripheral Visions: Learning along the Way*. New York: Harper Collins.

Begay, Lula M. (2002). *Awakened Belonging: Utilizing Traditional Stories to Enhance Self Perception of Dine Children*. Dissertation Abstracts International Section a: Humanities and Social Sciences, 63, 841.

Benham, M.K. & Heck, R.H. (1998). *Culture and Educational Policy in Hawai'i: The Silencing of Native Voices*. Mahwah, NJ: Lawrence Erlbaum.

Bigelow, Bill; Harvey, Brenda; Karp, Stan & Miller, Larry (Eds.). (2001). *Rethinking Our Classrooms: Teaching for Equity and Justice*. Milwaukee, WI: Rethinking Schools.

Bigelow, Bill & Peterson, Bob (2002). *Rethinking Globalization: Teaching for Justice in an Unjust World*. Milwaukee, WI: Rethinking Schools.

Blanton, Carlos Kevin (2004). *The Strange Career of Bilingual Education in Texas, 1836–1981*. College Station, TX: Texas A&M University Press.

Blaut, J. M. (1993). *The Colonizer's Model of the World*. New York: Guilford Press.

Bohn, Anita A. & Sleeter, Christine E. (2001). "Will Multicultural Education Survive the Standards Movement?" *Education Digest*. 66, 17–25.

Bravo, Marco A.; Hiebert, Elfrieda H. & Pearson, P. David (2007). "Tapping into the Linguistic Resources of Spanish/English Bilinguals: The Role of Cognates in Science," (pp. 140–156). In Richard K. Wagner, Andera E. Muse & Kendra R. Tannenbaum (Eds.). *Vocabulary Acquisition: Implications for Reading Comprehension*. New York: Guilford Press.

Burk, Nanci M. (2000). *Empowering At-Risk Students: Storytelling as a Pedagogical Tool*. (ED447497). Paper presented at the 86th Annual Meeting of the National Communication Association. Seattle, WA, November 9–12.

Butterworth, Susan & Lo Cicero, Anna Maria (2001). "Storytelling: Building a Mathematics Curriculum from the Culture of the Child." *Teaching Children Mathematics*. 7, 396–399.

Cammarota, J. & Romero, A. (2006). A critically compassionate intellectualism for Latina/o students: Raising voices above the silencing of our schools. *Multicultural Education*, 14 (2), 16–23.

Cantoni, Gina. P. (1999). "Using TPR-Storytelling to Develop Fluency and Literacy in Native American Languages," (pp. 53–58). In Jon Reyhner, Gina Cantoni, Robert N. St. Clair & Evangeline Parsons Yazzie (Eds.). *Revitalizing Indigenous Languages*. Flagstaff, AZ: Northern Arizona University.

Carroll, Shelia Dailey (1999). *Storytelling for Literacy*.(ED430234). Paper presented at the 43rd Annual Meeting of the Michigan Reading Association at Grand Rapids, MI, March 13–16.

Carruthers, Jacob H. (1994). "Black Intellectuals and the Crisis in Black Education," (pp. 37–55). In Mwalimu J. Shujaa (Ed.). *Too Much Schooling, Too Little Education: A Paradox of Black Life in White Societies*. Trenton, NJ: Africa World Press.

Carter, Kathy. (1993). "The Place of Story in the Study of Teaching and Teacher Education." *Educational Researcher.* 22, 5–12, 18.

Carter-Black, Janet (2007). "Teaching Cultural Competence: An Innovative Strategy Grounded in the Universality of Storytelling as Depicted in African and African American Storytelling Traditions." *Journal of Social Work Education.* 43, 31–50.

Center for Applied Linguistics (CAL) (January 13, 2001). *Arabic* Language Teaching in the United States.

Chacón, Justin Akers & Davis, Mike (2006). *No One is Illegal: Fighting Violence and State Repression on the U.S.—Mexico Border.* Chicago: Haymarket Books.

Chapman, L.H. (2007). An update on No Child Left Behind and national trends in education. *Arts Education Policy Review, 109(1),* 25–36.

Chomsky, Noam & Herman, Edward (1979). *The Washington Connection and Third World Fascism.* Boston, MA: South End Press.

Chomsky, Noam (1991). *Deterring Democracy.* New York: Verso Press.

Chomsky, Noam (1999). *Latin America: From Colonization to Globalization.* Melbourne, VIC: Ocean Press.

Chomsky, Noam (2000). *Chomsky on Miseducation.* Lanham, MD: Rowman & Littlefield.

Christensen, Linda (1995). "Whose Standard? Teaching Standard English in Our Schools," (pp. 128–135). In David Levine, Robert Lowe, Bob Peterson & Rita Tenorio (Eds.). *Rethinking Schools: An Agenda for Change.* New York: The New Press.

Clandinin, D. Jean & Connelly, F. Michael (1996). "Teachers' Professional Knowledge Landscapes: Teacher Stories—Stories of Teachers—School Stories—Stories of Schools." *Educational Researcher.* 25(3), 24–30.

Clark, Kenneth & Clark, Mamie (1939). "The Development of Consciousness of Self and the Emergence of Racial Identification in Negro Preschool Children." *Journal of Social Psychology.* 10, 591–599.

Collier, Virginia P.; Thomas, W. Wayne & Tinajero, Josefina (2006). "From Remediation to Enrichment: Transforming Texas Schools Through Dual Language Education." *TABE Journal.* 9, 23–34.

Connelly, F. Michael & Clandinin, D. Jean (2000). "Narrative Understandings of Teacher Knowledge." *Journal of Curriculum and Supervision.* 15, 315–331.

Connelly, F. Michael & Clandinin, D. Jean (1990). "Stories of Experience and Narrative Inquiry." *Educational Researcher.* 19, 2–14.

Connelly, Michael & Clandinin, D. Jean (Eds.). (1999). *Shaping a Professional Identity: Stories of Educational Practice.* New York: Teachers College Press.

Copenhaver-Johnson, J.F., Bowman, J.T., & Johnson, A.C. (2007). Santa-stories: Children's inquiry about race during picture-book read-alouds. *Language Arts,* 84(3), 234–244.

Costantino, Giuseppe & Malgady, Robert. G. (1996). "Culturally Sensitive Treatment: Cuento and Hero/Heroine Modeling Therapies for Hispanic Children and Adolescents," (pp. 639–669). In Euthymia D. Hibbs & Peter S. Jensen (Eds.). *Psychosocial Treatments for Child and Adolescent Disorders: Empirically Based Strategies for Clinical Practice.* Washington, DC: American Psychological Association.

Constantino, Renato (1978). *Neocolonial Identity and Counter Consciousness: Essays on Cultural Decolonization.* London: Merlin Press.

Cowell, Andrew (2002). "Bilingual Curriculum among the Northern Arapaho." *American Indian Quarterly*. 26, 24–43.

Crawford, James (2000). *At War With Diversity: U.S. Language Policy in an Age of Anxiety*. Tonawanda, NY: Multilingual Matters.

Crenshaw, Kimberle Williams (1995). "Race, Reform, and Retrenchment: Transformation and Legitimation in Anti-discrimination," (pp. 103–122). In Kimberle Crenshaw, Neil Gotanda, Gary Peller & Kendall Thomas (Eds.). *Critical Race Theory: The Key Writings That Formed the Movement*. New York: The New Press.

Cross, William E. (1991). *Shades of Black, Diversity in African American Identity*. Philadelphia, PA: Temple University Press.

Cruz-Janzen, Marta. I. (2002). "Lives on the Crossfire: The Struggle of Multiethnic and Multiracial Latinos for Identity in a Dichotomous and Racialized World." *Race, Gender & Class*. 9, 47–62.

Cummins, Jim (1996). *Negotiating Identities: Education for Empowerment in a Diverse Society*. Ontario, CA: California Association for Bilingual Education.

Cummins, Jim (2005). "A Proposal for Action: Strategies for Recognizing Heritage Language Competence as a Learning Resource within the Mainstream Classroom." *The Modern Language Journal*. 89, 585–592.

Dalley-Trim, L. (2006). 'Just boys being boys'? *Youth Studies Australia*, 25(3), 26–33.

Darder, Antonia (1991). *Culture and Power in the Classroom*. Westport, CT: Bergin & Garvey.

de Burgos, Julia (1982). *Canción de la Yerdad Sencilla* (2nd ed.). Río Piedras, PR: Ediciones Huracán.

de Burgos, Julia & Agüeros, Jack (1997). *Song of the Simple Truth : Obra Completa Poética: The Complete Poems* (1st ed.). Willimantic, CT: Curbstone Press.

Delpit, Lisa (1995). *Other People's Children: Cultural Conflict in the Classroom*. New York: The New Press.

Derman-Sparks, Louise (1985). "How Well are We Nurturing Racial and Ethnic Diversity?" (pp. 17–22). In Robert Lowe, Robert Peterson, David Levine & Rita Tenorio (Eds.). *Rethinking Schools: An Agenda for Change*. New York: The New Press.

Derman-Sparks, Louise; Higa, Christina & Sparks, B. (1980). "Children, Race and Racism: How Race Awareness Develops." *Interracial Books for Children Bulletin*. 11(3&4).http://www.nncc.org/Diversity/dc31_celebrate.divers.html.

Dorris, Michael (1998). "Why I'm Not Thankful for Thanksgiving," (p. 76) In Bill Bigelow & Bob Peterson (Eds.). *Rethinking Columbus: The Next 500 Years*. Milwaukee, WI: Rethinking Schools.

Duncan-Owens, D. (2008, June 4). Evidentiary sleight of hand: The high stakes of silencing teachers. *Online Submission*, (ERIC Document Reproduction Service No. ED501572) Retrieved September 23, 2008, from ERIC Database.

Dowdy, Joanne Kilgour (2002). "Oyuh Dyuh," (pp. 3–13). In Lisa Delpit & Joanne Kilgour Dowdy (Eds.). *The Skin That We Speak: Thoughts on Language and Culture in the Classroom*. New York: The New Press.

Dworin, Joel (2003). "Insights into Biliteracy Development: Toward a Bidirectional Theory of Bilingual Pedagogy." *Journal of Hispanic Higher Education*. 2, 171–186.

Elenes, C. Alejandra; Gonzalez, F.; Delgado Bernal, Dolores & Villenas, Sofia (2001). "Introduction: Chicana/Mexicana Feminist Pedagogies: Consejos, Respeto, y Educacion in Everyday Life." *Qualitative Studies in Education.* 14, 595–602.

Eldridge, F. (1957). "Helping Hands from Mexico." *Saturday Evening Post.* 230, 28–64.

Elliott, Andrea (2006). "For Recruiter Speaking Arabic, Saying Go Army Is a Hard Job." *New York Times,* October 7.

Esquivel, A., Lewis, K. Rodriquez, D. Stovall, D., & Williams, T. (2002). We know what's best for you: Silencing of people of color. In Slater, Fain, and Rossatto (Eds), *The Freirean Legacy: Educating for Social Justice* (pp. 207–219). New York: Peter Lang Publishing.

Fanon, Frantz (2004). *The Wretched of the Earth.* Introduction by Jean-Paul Sartre & Homi K. Bhabha. New York: Grove Press.

Feagin, Joe R. (1991). "The Continuing Significance of Race: Antiblack Discrimination in Public Places." *American Sociological Review.* 56, 101–116.

Ferdman, Bernado M. & Gallego, P. (2001). "Racial Identity Development and Latinos in the United States," In Charmaine L. Wijeyesinghe & Bailey W. Jackson III (Eds.). *New Perspectives on Racial Identity Development: A Theoretical and Practical Anthology.* New York, New York University Press, 32–66.

Fine, Michelle; Weiss, Lois; Pruitt, Linda Powell & Burns, April (1997). *Off White: Readings on Power, Privilege and Resistance.* New York: Routledge.

Fishman, Joshua (Spring, 2000). "English: The Killer Language? Or a Passing Phase?" *WholeEarth.* 100. http://www.wholeearth.com/issue/2100/article/139/english.the.killer.language.or.a.passing.phase

Fishman, Joshua (Winter, 1998). "The New linguistic Order: What Stands in the Way of the Global Spread of English? Some Dyspeptic French Culturecrats? A Few Hundred Million Chinese? Given How Greatly English Has Profited from Globalization, It seems Inevitable That They'll Come Around, Right? Au Contraire: English Will Have Its Run, But the Future is Multilingual." *Foreign Policy.* 113, 26–40.

Foucault, Michel (1984). *The Foucault Reader.* (Rabinow, Paul, Ed.). New York: Pantheon Books.

Freire, Paulo (1970). *Pedagogy of the Oppressed.* New York: Continuum.

Freire, Paulo (1985). *The Politics of Education: Culture Power and Liberation.* South Hadley, MA: Bergen & Garvey.

Freire, Paulo (1998a). *Teachers as Cultural Workers: Letters to Those Who Dare to Teach.* Boulder, CO: Westview Press.

Freire, Paulo (1998b). *Pedagogy of Freedom: Ethics, Democracy and Civic Courage.* Lanham, MD: Rowman & Littlefield.

Freire, Paulo (2000). *Pedagogy of the Oppressed.* (Myra Bergman Ramos, Trans. 30th Anniversary Edition). New York: Continuum.

Freire, Paulo & Macedo, Denaldo (1987). *Literacy: Reading the Word and the World.* South Hadley, MA: Bergen & Garvey.

Fusco, Coco (1995). *English is Broken Here.* New York: The New Press.

Futrell, Mary Hatwood & Witty, Elaine P. (1997). "Preparation and Professional Development of Teachers for Culturally Diverse Schools: Perspectives from the Standards Movement," (pp. 189–216). In Jacqueline Jordan Irvine (Ed.). *Critical Knowledge for Diverse Teachers and*

Learners. Washington, DC: American Association of Colleges for Teachers Education.

Galindo, Rene & Olguin, Monica (1996). "Reclaiming Bilingual Educators' Cultural Resources: An Autobiographical Approach." *Urban Education.* 31, 29–56.

García, Ofelia & Bartlett, Leslie (2007). "A Speech Community Model of Bilingual Education: Educating Latino Newcomers in the USA." *International Journal of Bilingual Education & Bilingualism.* 10, 1–25.

Gay, Geneva (2000). *Culturally Responsive Teaching: Theory, Research, and Practice.* New York: Teachers College Press.

Giroux, Henry A. (1988). *Teachers as Intellectuals: Toward a Critical Pedagogy of Learning.* Westport, CT: Bergin & Garvey.

Goldstein, L. S. (1997). *Teaching with Love: A Feminist Approach to Early Childhood Education.* New York: Peter Lang.

Goleman, Daniel (1995). *Emotional Intelligence.* New York: Bantam Books.

Gonzalez, Norm (2005). *I Am My Language.* Tucson, AZ: The University of Arizona Press.

González Baker, S. (1996). "Demographic Trends in the Chicana/o Population: Policy Implications for the Twenty-First Century," (pp. 5–24). In David R. Maciel & Isidro D. Ortiz (Eds.). *Chicanas/Chicanos at the Crossroads: Social, Economic, and Political Change.* Tucson, AZ: The University of Arizona Press.

Gotanda, Neil (1995). "A Critique of 'Our Constitution is Color-Blind,'" (pp. 257–275). In Kimberle Crenshaw, Neil Gotanda, Gary Peller & Kendall Thomas (Eds.). *Critical Race Theory: The Key Writings That Formed the Movement.* New York: The New Press.

Grant, Carl A. (1997). "Critical Knowledge, Skills, and Experiences for the Instruction of Culturally Diverse Students: A Perspective for the Preparation of Preservice Teachers," (pp. 1–26). In Jacqueline Jordan Irvine (Ed.). *Critical Knowledge for Diverse Teachers and Learners.* Washington, DC: The American Association of Colleges for Teacher Education.

Grant, Madison & Davison, Stewart (Eds.). (1928). *The Founders of the Republic on Immigration, Naturalization and Aliens.* New York: Scribner.

Gutierrez, David (1977). *Walls and Mirrors: Mexican American, Mexican Immigrants and the Politics of Ethnicity.* University of California Press.

Gutierrez, Ramon (2003). "Ethnic Mexicans in Historical and Social Science Scholarship," (pp. 261–287). In James A. Banks & Cherry A. McGee Banks (Eds.). *Handbook of Research on Multicultural Education.* San Francisco, CA: Jossey-Bass.

Gutierrez, Kris D. & Jaramillo, Nathalia E. (2006). "Looking for Educational Equity: The Consequences of Relying on Brown," (pp. 173–189). In Arnetha Ball (Ed.). *With More Deliberate Speed: Achieving Equity and Excellence in Education-Realizing the Full Potential of Brown V.* Board of Education Part II (Yearbook. National Society for the Study of Education, New York). http://nsse-chicago.org.

Hale-Benson, Janice E. (1982). *Black Children: Their Roots, Culture, and Learning Styles.* Baltimore, MD: The John Hopkins University Press.

Hankins, K. (1999). Silencing the lambs. In J. Allen (Ed.), *Class Actions: Teaching for Social Justice in Elementary and Middle School* (p. 61–71). New York: Teachers College Press.

Harding, Vincent (1990). *Hope and History: Why We Must Share the Story of the Movement.* Maryknoll, NY: Orbis Books.

Harjo, Susan Shown (1998). "We Have No Reason to Celebrate an Invasion," (p. 4). In Bill

Bigelow & Bob Peterson (Eds.). *Rethinking Columbus: The Next 500 Years*. Milwaukee, WI: Rethinking Schools.

He, Ming Fang & Phillion, Joann (Eds.). (2008). *Personal~Passionate~Participatory Inquiry Into Social Justice in Education*. Charlotte, NC: Information Age Publishing.

Heinicke, Craig & Grove, Wayne A. (2005) "Labor Markets, Regional Diversity, and Cotton Harvest Mechanization in the Post-World War II United States." *Social Science History*. 29, 269–297.

Helms, Janet E. & Cook, Donelda A. (1999). *Using Race and Culture in Counseling and Psychotherapy: Theory and Process*. Needham Heights, MA: Allyn & Bacon.

Hill, Stacie; Gómez, Richard & Gómez, Leo (2008). "What a Difference a Year Makes: A Large Urban School District's Transformation from Remedial to an Enrichment Dual Language Education." *TABE Journal*. 10, 154–177.

Holland, Dorothy; Lachicotte, Jr., William; Skinner, Debra & Cain, Carole (1998). *Identity and Agency in Cultural Worlds*. Cambridge, MA: Harvard University Press.

hooks, bell (2000). *Where We Stand: Class Matter*. New York: Routledge.

hooks, bell (1994). *Teaching to Transgress: Education as a Practice of Freedom*. New York: Routledge.

Horton, Myles & Freire, Paulo (1990). *We Make the Road by Walking: Conversations On Education and Social Change*. (Brenda Bell, John Gaventa & John Peter, Eds.). Philadelphia, PA: Temple University Press.

Howard, Elizabeth (1997). *Teachers' Beliefs About Effective Educational Practices For Language-Minority Students: A Case Study, Qualifying Paper*. Cambridge, MA: Harvard Graduate School of Education.

Irvine, Jacqueline Jordan (Ed.). (2003). *Critical Knowledge for Diverse Teachers and Learners*. Washington, DC: American Association of Colleges for Teacher Education.

Jackson, F. (1999). The impact of "dysconscious racism." *Multicultural Perspectives*, 1 (4), 15–18.

Jenlink, Patrick. (2006). "Learning Our Identity as Teacher–Teacher Identity as Palimpsest." *Teacher Education & Practice*. 19, 118–130.

Jennings, Francis (1975). *The Invasion of America: Indians, Colonialism, and the Cant of Conquest*. Chapel Hill, NC: University of South Carolina Press.

Jolongo, Mary Renck & Isenberg, Joan P. (1995). *Teaching Stories: From Personal Narrative to Professional Insight*. San Francisco, CA: Jossey-Bass.

Johnson, S., Berg, H., Donaldson, M.L. (2005). *Who stays in teaching and why: A review of the literature*. NRTA' Education Support Network: Harvard Graduate School of Education.

Juenke, Eric Gonzalez (2004). *Macro-Economic Labor Conditions and Latino Students How Unemployment Changes Affect Dropout Rates*. The Project for Equity Representation and Governance, Texas A&M University. http://teep.tamu.edu/reports/report026.pdf.

Katz, Karen (2007). *The Colors of Us*. New York: Henry Holt.

Kellas, Jody Koenig (2005). "Family Ties: Communicating Identity through Jointly Told Family Stories." *Communication Monographs*. 72, 365–389.

Kharem, Haroon (2006). *A Curriculum of Repression: A Pedagogy of Racial History in the United States*. New York: Peter Lang.

Kincheloe, Joe L. (2003). *Teachers as Researchers: Qualitative Inquiry as a Path to Empowerment*. New York: RoutledgeFalmer.

Kendrick, M. & McKay, R. (2002). Uncovering literacy narratives through children's drawings.

Canadian Journal of Education, 27(1), 45–60.

Koki, Stan (1998). *Storytelling: The Heart and Soul of Education. PREL Briefing Paper.* Honolulu, HI: Pacific Resources for Education and Learning.

Kozol, Jonathan (2005). *The Shame of the Nation: The Restoration of Apartheid Schooling in America.* New York: Crown Publishers.

Ladson-Billings, Gloria (Ed.). (2003). *Critical Race Theory: Perspectives on the Social Studies: The Profession, Policies, and Curriculum.* Greenwich, CT: Information Age Publishing.

Ladson-Billings, Gloria (2001). *Crossing Over to Canaan: The Journey of New Teachers in Diverse Classrooms.* San Francisco, CA: Jossey-Bass.

Ladson-Billings, Gloria (1999). "Preparing Teachers for Diverse Student Populations: A Critical Race Theory Perspective." *Review of Research in Education.* 24, 211–247.

Ladson-Billings, Gloria (1997). "I don't See Color, I Just See Children: Dealing with Stereotyping and Prejudice in Young Children," In Mary E. Haas & Margaret A. Laughlin (Eds.). *Meeting the Standards: Social Studies Readings for K-6 Educators.* Washington, DC: National Council for the Social Studies, 305–308.

Laird, J., DeBell, M., Kienzl, G. & Chapman, C. (2007). *Dropout Rates in the United States: 2005* (NCES 2007–059). U.S. Department of Education. Washington, DC: National Center for Education Statistics. Retrieved May 25, 2009 from http://nces.ed.gov/pubsearch

Lastra, Sarai (1999). "Juan Bobo: A Folkloric Information System." *Library Trends.* 47, 529–557.

Lawrence, Charles R., III (1995). "The Id, the Ego, and Equal Protection: Reckoning with Unconscious Racism," (pp. 235–257). In Kimberle Crenshaw, Neil Gotanda, Gary Peller & Kendall Thomas (Eds.). *Critical Race Theory: The Key Writings That Formed the Movement.* New York: The New Press.

Leseho, Johanna & Block, Laurie. (2005). "'Listen and I Tell You Something': Storytelling and Social Action in the Healing of the Oppressed." *British Journal of Guidance and Counselling.* 33, 175–184.

Livo, Norma J. & Reitz, Sandra A.(1986). *Storytelling: Process and Practice.* Littleton, CO: Libraries Unlimited.

Llorens, M.B. (1994). Action Research: Are Teachers Finding Their Voice? *The Elementary School Journal,* 95 (1), 3–10.

Loewen, James W. (2007). *Lies My Teacher Told Me: Everything Your American History Textbook Got Wrong.* New York: Simon & Schuster.

Lopez, A. & Hall, M. (2007). Letting in the sun: Native youth transform their school with murals. *Reclaiming Children and Youth,* 16 (3), 29–35.

Loury, Glenn C. (2002). *The Anatomy of Racial Inequality.* Cambridge, MA: Harvard University Press.

Macedo, Donaldo. (1994). *Literacies of Power: What Americans Are Not Allowed to Know,* expanded edition. Boulder, CO: Westview Press.

Macedo, Donaldo. (2000). "The Colonialism of the English Only Movement." *Educational Researcher.* 29, 15–24.

Macedo, Donaldo & Bartolomé, Lilia I.(1999). *Dancing with Bigotry: Beyond the Politics of Tolerance.* New York: St. Martin's Press.

Macias, Jose (1996). "Resurgence of Ethnic Nationalism in California and Germany: The Impact on Recent Progress in Education." *Anthropology & Education Quarterly.* 27, 232–252.

Mankiller, W. (2004). *Everyday is a Good Day: Reflections by Contemporary Indigenous Women.* Golden, CO: Fulcrum Publishing.

Matthews, M.W. & Kesner, J.E. (2000). The silencing of Sammy: One struggling reader learning with his peers. *The Reading Teacher, 53(5),* 382–390.

Meiden, W. (1958). "The Development of Fluency in Foreign Language Courses." *Modern Language Journal.* 42(2), 82–86.

Memmi, Albert (1965). *The Colonizer and the Colonized.* Boston, MA: Beacon Press.

Merk, Frederick (1963). *Manifest Destiny and Mission in American History: A Reinterpretation.* New York: Vintage Books.

Miller, Peggy J., Fung, Heidi & Chian-Hui, Eva (1997). "Personal Storytelling as a Medium of Socialization in Chinese and American Families." *Child Development.* 68(3), 557–568.

Moll, L. C., González, N. & Amanti, C. (2005). *Funds of Knowledge: Theorizing Practices in Households, Communities, and Classrooms.* Mahwah, NJ: Lawrence Erlbaum.

Montero-Sieburth, Martha & Pérez, Marla (1987). "Echar pa 'lante, Moving Onward: The Dilemmas and Strategies of a Bilingual Teacher." *Anthropology & Education Quarterly.* 18, 180–189.

Murrell, Peter C., Jr. (2001). *The Community Teacher: A New Framework for Effective Urban Teaching.* New York: Teachers College Press.

National Commission on Excellence in Education (1983). *A Nation at Risk: The Imperative for Educational Reform: A Report to the Nation and the Secretary of Education. United States Department of Education.* http://www.ed.gov/pubs/NatAtRisk/risk.html.

Natriello, Gary & Pallas, Aaron M. (2001). "The Development and Impact of High-Stakes Testing," (pp. 19–38). In Gary Orfield & Mindy L. Kornhaber (Eds.). *Raising Standards or Raising Barriers? Inequality and High-Stakes Testing in Public Education.* New York: The Century Foundation Press.

Nieto, S. (2003). *What Keeps Teachers Going?* New York: Teachers College Press.

Nieto, Sonia & Bode, Patricia (2008). *Affirming Diversity: The Sociopolitical Context of Multicultural Education* (5th ed.). New York: Pearson Education.

New York City Department of Education (2006). *Chancellor's Regulations: Promotion Standards.* Retrieved October 10, 2006 from http://docs.nycenet.edu/docushare/dsweb/Get/Document-24/A-501.pdf.

Ng, Jennifer C. (2003). "Teacher Shortages in Urban Schools: The Role of Traditional and Alternative Certification Routes in Filling the Void." *Education and Urban Society.* 35(4), 380–398.

Osa, Osayimwense (1997). "Traditional African Informal Instructional Paradigm in African and African American Children's Literature." *Western Journal of Black Studies.* 21, 280–289.

Paley, Vivian Gussin (1989). *White Teacher.* Cambridge, MA: Harvard University Press.

Palmer, Parker J. (1998). *The Courage to Teach: Exploring the Inner Landscape of a Teacher's Life.* San Francisco, CA: Jossey-Bass.

Peller, Gary (1995). "Race-Consciousness," (pp. 127–158). In Kimberle Crenshaw, Neil Gotanda, Gary Peller & Kendall Thomas (Eds.). *Critical Race Theory: The Key Writings That Formed the Movement.* New York: The New Press.

Pennycook, A. (1998). *English and the Discourses of Colonialism.* New York: Routledge.

Pettus, Ashley (2007). "End of the Melting Pot? The New Wave of Immigrants Presents New

Challenges." *Harvard Magazine.* 105, 44–53.

Phillipson, R; Rannut, M & Skutnabb-Kangas, T. (1995). "Introduction," (pp. 1–24). In Tove Skutnabb-Kangas, Robert Phillipson & Mart Rannut (Eds.). *Linguistic Human Rights: Overcoming Linguistic Discrimination.* New York: Mouton de Gruyter.

Piquemal, Nathalie (2003). "From Native North American Oral Traditions to Western Literacy: Storytelling in Education." *Alberta Journal of Educational Research.* 49, 113–122.

Pickford, Steve (2005). "Emerging Pedagogies of Linguistic and Cultural Continuity in Papua New Guinea." *Language, Culture and Curriculum.* 18, 139–153.

Portales, Marco (2000). *Crowding Out Latinos- Mexican Americans in the Public Consciousness.* Philadelphia, PA: Temple University Press.

Quiocho, Alice & Rios, Francisco (2000). "The Power of Their Presence: Minority Group Teachers and Schooling." *Review of Education Research.* 70, 485–528.

Rains, Frances (2003). "To Greet the Dawn with Open Eyes: American Indians, White Privilege and the Power of Residual Guilt in the Social Studies," (pp. 199–227). In Gloria Ladson-Billings (Ed.). *Critical Race Theory Perspectives on the Social Studies: The Profession, Polices and Curriculum.* Greenwich, CT: Information Publishing.

Razib (2008a). "On Human Genetic Variation and Human Identity." January 16, *Anthropology.Net.* http://anthropology.net/2008/01/16/on-human-genetic-variation-and-human-identity/

Razib (2008b). "Skin Color is a Deceptive Character." January 31, *Gene Expression.* http://www.gnxp.com/blog/2008/01/skin-color-is-deceptive-character.php.

Reagan, Timothy (2002). *Language, Education, and Ideology: Mapping the Landscape of U.S. Schools.* Westport, CT: Praeger.

Revilla, Anita Tijerina, Wells, Amy Stuart & Holme, Jennifer Jellison (2004). "'We Didn't See Color': The Salience of Color Blindness in Desegregated Schools," (pp. 284–301). In Michelle Fine, Lois Weis, Linda Powell Pruitt & April Burns (Eds.). *Off White: Readings on Power, Privilege, and Resistance.* (2nd ed.). New York: Routledge.

Richardson, Virginia (1994). "Conducting Research on Practice." *Educational Researcher.* 23, 5–10.

Rodriguez, Dalia. (2006). "Un/masking Identity: Healing Our Wounded Souls." *Qualitative Inquiry.* 12, 1067–1090.

Rodriguez, Clara E. (2000). *Changing Race: Latinos, the Census, and the History of Ethnicity in the United States.* New York: New York University Press.

Rodriguez, Clara. E. (1996). "Racial Themes in the Literature: Puerto Ricans and Other Latinos," (pp. 105–125). In Gabriel B. Haslip-Viera & Sherrie L. Baver (Eds.). *Latinos in New York: Communities in Transition.* Notre Dame, IN: University of Notre Dame Press.

Romo, David Dorado (2005). *Ringside Seat to a Revolution: An Underground Cultural History of El Paso and Juarez: 1893–1923.* El Paso, TX: Cinco Puntos Press.

Romo, Harriet D. & Falbo, Toni (1996). *Latino High School Graduation: Defying the Odds.* Austin, TX: University of Texas Press.

Roy, Arundhati (2004). *An Ordinary Person's Guide to Empire.* Cambridge, MA: South End Press.

Rubal-Lopez, Alma (1994). "The Linguistic Acculturation of Puerto Ricans in the United States," (pp. 327–337). In A. Monadaco Lorenzo, Carmen Flys Junquera & Jose Antonio Palacios (Eds.). *El poder Hispano: Actas del V Congreso de Culturas* . Madrid: Universidad de

Alcala.

Rymes, Betsy (2001). *Conversational Borderlands: Language and Identity in an Alternative Urban High School*. New York: Teachers College Press.

Saavedra, Elizabeth (1995). *Teacher Transformation: Creating Texts and Contexts in Study Groups*. Unpublished manuscript. Tucson, AZ: University of Arizona.

Schneider, J.J. (2001). No Blood, Guns, or Gays Allowed! The Silencing of the Elementary Writer. *Language Arts*, 78(5), 415–425.

Schofield, Janet Ward (1997). "Causes and Consequences of the Colorblind Perspective," (pp. 251–271). In James A. Banks & Cherry A. McGee Banks (Eds.). *Multicultural Education: Issues and Perspectives* (3rd ed.), Boston, MA: Allyn & Bacon.

Scott, James C. (1990). *Domination and the Art of Resistance: Hidden Transcripts*. New Haven, CT: Yale University Press.

Scripca, Dana (2004). *White Asian Skin against Tanning*. Retrieved July 7, 2008. http://www.safe-tan.com.au/articles/White_Asian_Skin_Against_Tanning.htm

Simon, N. (1993). *Why Am I Different?* New York: Whitman.

Sfard, A. & Prusak, A. (2005). Telling Identities: In Search of an Analytic Tool for Investigating Learning as a Culturally Shaped Activity. *Educational Researcher*, 34(4), 14–22 .

Simpson, Howard N. (1980). *Invisible Armies: The Impact of Diseases on American History*. Indianapolis, IN: Bobbs-Merrill.

Skutnabb-Kangas, Tove (2000). *Linguistic Genocide in Education—or Worldwide Diversity and Human Rights?* Mahwah, NJ: Lawrence Erlbaum.

Skutnabb-Kangas, Tove (1989). *Bilingualism or Not: The Education of Minorities*. Clevedon, England: Multilingual Matters.

Smith, Linda Tuhiwai (1999). *Decolonizing Methodologies: Research and Indigenous Peoples*. New York: Zed Books.

Solorzano, Daniel G. (1997). "Images and Words That Wound: Critical Race Theory, Racial Stereotyping, and Teacher Education." *Teacher Education Quarterly*. 24, 5–19.

Solorzano, Daniel G. (1998). "Critical Race Theory, Race and Gender Microaggressions, and the Experience of Chicana and Chicano Scholars." *International Journal of Qualitative Studies in Education*. 11, 121–136.

Soto, Lourdes Diaz (2002a). "Young Bilingual Children's Perceptions of Bilingualism and Biliteracy: Altruistic Possibilities." *Bilingual Research Journal*. 26, 599–610.

Soto, Lourdes Diaz (Ed.) (2002b). *Making a Difference in the Lives of Bilingual/Bicultural Children*. New York: Peter Lang.

Soto, Lourdes Diaz (1997). *Language, Culture, and Power. Bilingual Families and the Struggle for Quality Education*. New York: SUNY Press.

Spring, Joel (2005). *Conflicts of Interests: The Politics of American Education*. New York: McGraw-Hill.

Spring, Joel (2001). *Deculturalization and the Struggle for Equality: A Brief History of the Education of Dominated Cultures in the United States*. Boston, MA: McGraw-Hill.

Steinberg, Shirley & Kincheloe, Joe (Eds.). (2004). *19 Urban Questions: Teaching in the City*. New York: Peter Lang.

Stephanson, Anders (1995). *Manifest Destiny: American Expansion and the Empire of Right*. New York: Hill & Wang.

Stern, Daniel (1985). *The Interpersonal World of the Infant.* New York: Harper

Stonequist, Everett V. (1961). *The Marginal Man: A Study in Personality and Culture Conflict.* New York: Russell & Russell.

Stubbs, Michael (2002). "Some Basic Sociolinguistic Concepts," (pp. 63–85). In Lisa Delpit & Joanne Kilgour Dowdy (Eds.). *The Skin That We Speak: Thoughts on Language and Culture in the Classroom.* New York: The New Press.

Sunshine, Catherine A. & Warner, Keith O. (Eds.). (1998). *Caribbean Connections: Moving North.* Washington, DC: Network of Educators on the Americas.

Tappan, Mark B. & Packer, Martin J. (Eds.). (1991). *Narrative and Storytelling: Implications for Understanding Moral Development.* San Francisco, CA: Jossey-Bass.

Taylor, J.M., Gilligan, C., & Sullivan, A.M. (1995). *Between Voice and Silence: Women and Girls, Race and Relationship.* Cambridge, MA: Harvard University Press.

Torres-Guzman, María E. (2002). "Dual Language Programs: Key Features and Results." *Directions-National Clearinghouse for Bilingual Education.* 14, 1–16.

Urrieta, Luis, Jr. (2004a). "'Assistencialism' and the Politics of High-Stakes Testing." *The Urban Review.* 36, 211–226.

Urrieta, Luis, Jr. (2004b). "Dis-Connections in 'American' Citizenship and the Post/Neo-Colonial: People of Mexican Descent and Whitestream Pedagogy and Curriculum." *Theory and Research in Social Education.* 32(4), 433–458.

Urrieta, Luis, Jr. (2005). "'Playing the Game' Versus 'Selling Out': Chicanas and Chicanos Relationship to Whitestream Schools," pp. 165–190. In Bryant Keith Alexander, Gary L. Anderson & Bernardo Gallegos (Eds.). *Performance Theories in Education: Power, Pedagogy, and the Politics of Identity.* Mahwah, NJ: Lawrence Erlbaum.

Valdes, Guadalupe. (1997). "Dual Language Immersion Programs: A Cautionary Note Concerning the Education of Language-Minority Students." *Harvard Educational Review.* 67(3), 391–429.

Valencia, Richard (Ed.). (2002). *Chicano School Failure and Success: Past, Present, and Future* (2nd ed.). New York: Routledge.

Valencia, Richard (2005). "The Mexican American Struggle for Equal Educational Opportunity in Mendez v. Westminster: Helping to Pave the Way for Brown v Board of Education." *Teachers College Record.* 107(3), 389–423.

Valenzuela, Angela (1999). *Subtractive Schooling: U.S.-Mexican Youth and the Politics of Caring.* New York: State University of New York.

Villanueva, Victor (1993). *Bootstraps: From an American Academic of Color.* Urbana, IL: National Council of Teachers of English.

West, Cornel (1994). *Race Matters.* New York: Vintage Books.

Weiner, Lois (1999). *Urban Teaching: The Essentials.* New York: Teachers College Press.

Winant, Howard (1994). *Racial Conditions.* Minneapolis, MN: University of Minnesota Press.

Winter, Jonah (1991). *Diego.* New York: Scholastic.

Wray, J. (Ed.). (2002). *Native Peoples of the Olympic Peninsula: Who We Are.* Norman, OK: University of Oklahoma Press.

Yellow Bird, Michael (1999). "Indian, American Indian, and Native Americans: Counterfeit Identities." *Winds of Change: A Magazine for American Indian Education and Opportunity.* 14, 1.

Zalaquett, Carlos P. & Lopez, A. D. (2006). "Learning From the Stories of Successful Undergraduate Latina/Latino Students: The Importance of Mentoring." *Mentoring & Tutoring: Partnership in Learning.* 14(3), 337–353.

Zeichner, K. and Hoeft, K (1996). Teacher Education and Cultural Diversity. In J. Sikula, T. Buttery, E. Guyton (Eds.). *Handbook on Research on Teacher Education,* 52 (4), 266–282.

Zentella, Ana Celia (1997). *Growing Up Bilingual: Puerto Rican Children in New York.* Malden, MA: Blackwell.

Zinn, Howard & Macedo, Donald (2005). *On Democratic Education.* Boulder, CO: Paradigm.

Zinn, Howard (2003). *A People's History of the United States: 1492-Present.* 20th edition. New York: HarperCollins.

Zweigenhaf, Richard L. & Domhoff, G. William (1991). *Blacks in the White Establishment? A Study of Race and Class in America.* New Haven, CT: Yale University Press.

Contributors

MERCEDES F. CEPEDA, currently an admissions counselor-instructor at Fashion Institute of Technology, was born in the Dominican Republic. After receiving her B.A. in History and Sociology with a concentration in Latin American and Caribbean Area Studies from Binghamton University, she completed her Masters of Science in Childhood Education from Brooklyn College. During her professional career, Mercedes has taught middle school social studies, sixth grade humanities, and elementary reading and writing in Brooklyn, New York.

GENEVIEVE COLLURA has worked as a teacher in Brooklyn, NY, for five years. She enjoys writing and publishing poetry, and conducts an after school painting club for fifth graders. She has worked in writing centers to edit papers and help English language learners, and has taught in college settings in her spare time.

ANTONIA DARDER is a distinguished professor of Educational Policy Studies and Latina/Latino Studies at the University of Illinois Urbana Champaign. She is the author of a variety of books and articles that examine the relationship between culture, language, racism, and schooling. Among these are *Culture and Power in the Classroom, Reinventing Paulo Freire: A Pedagogy of Love, and After Race: Racism After Multiculturalism*. Darder is also an activist, poet, and artist. Born in Puerto Rico and raised in East Angeles, her work is grounded in the struggle for social justice, human rights and economic democracy.

LENA BOUSTANI DARWICH is Assistant Professor, Education Department, Faculty of Literature and Humanities, GLOBAL University, Beirut, Lebanon, and Senior Lecturer, Department of Educational Foundations and Leadership, College of Education, University of Akron, Ohio. Dr. Darwich worked extensively with Public K-12 students of diverse backgrounds and with in-service and pre-service teachers both in the U.S. and the Middle East. Her research interests have included a focus on the manner in which internet resources can be used to enhance communication between diverse students and their teachers and on cultural dialogue amongst college students of diverse cultural and religious backgrounds. Dr. Darwich is currently researching the expectations of diverse women in higher education as related to mentorship, professional development, sense of efficacy and motivation, and leadership. Her latest work aims to tell the stories of Muslim women students as pre-service teachers, their challenges, their successes and their expectations. These women's stories present their perspectives on transforming teacher education to become more inclusive, specifically of women of diverse religious backgrounds, by challenging ingrained stereotyped assumptions.

IRENE GARZA undertook the task of going back to academic life (after having raised three bilingual/bicultural children) and received a Bachelor of Science in Applied Learning and Development with a Bilingual/ESL Specialization and minor in Spanish from the University of Texas at Austin. The experience and knowledge she obtained from teaching mainly Mexican immigrant children at the elementary level led her to expand her knowledge about the diverse experiences Mexican immigrant children face in the American school system. She continued expanding her knowledge about how to best meet the needs of this group of immigrant students and received a Master of Education with a specialization in multicultural studies from the University of Texas at Austin in 2006. Currently, she is attending the University of Texas at Austin pursuing a Ph. D. in Bilingual/Bicultural Education, while working part-time as an Assistant Instruction teaching in the Curriculum and Education Department at the University.

NOELLE GENTILE previously worked as a teaching artist throughout Brooklyn and as a classroom teacher. Currently, Ms. Gentile works as a drama teacher in a public elementary school in New York City. She has developed curriculum to foster and encourage students to create artistic work and expression through the lens of social justice and social action.

SHEILA BERNAL GUZMÁN is a lecturer at the University of Texas at Austin and a bilingual ESL program specialist for Elgin Independent School District. She received her doctorate in Educational Administration at The University of Texas at Austin. Her research interests include school improvement and dual language education.

SHARON L. HIXON taught first and second grades in Baltimore City Schools. At the college level, she has taught Developmental Reading at Frederick Community College and Dalton State College. Currently, she is an Associate Professor in the School of Education at Dalton State College in Dalton, Georgia. Her Ph.D. is from the University of Tennessee at Knoxville.

LINDA GUARDIA JACKSON is a lecturer at the University of Texas at San Antonio and a bilingual/ESL educational consultant for Jackson & Associates. She received her doctorate in Curriculum and Instruction in the area of Cultural Studies in Education at The University of Texas at Austin with a doctoral portfolio in Mexican American Studies. Her research interests and publications focus on the identity-making of Latina teachers and autobiographical storytelling.

HAROON KHAREM is an Associate Professor of Education at Brooklyn College. He has been teaching African American history at Performing Arts & Technology High School (PATHS) in Brooklyn for the past four years. Kharem taught and mentored numerous Teaching Fellows and is a scholar of African American history and studies. His recent book is *Education As Freedom: African American Educational Thought and Activism.* His recent articles deal with images of African Americans in education and the Moors in Spain. He is currently working on a book on the African Americans and the African Free Schools in New York City Antebellum Period.

FRANCES V. RAINS, Ph.D. (Choctaw/Cherokee & Japanese) is an Associate Professor in the Native American and World Indigenous Peoples Studies at Evergreen State College. Her research interests include Indigenous Knowledge, white privilege/racism, Native Women, environmental and social justice issues. Her recent publications include: "Even When Erased, We Exist: Native Women Standing Strong for Justice," which was published in Caracciolo & Mungai (Eds.) *In the Spirit of Ubuntu; Stories of Teaching & Research,* (2009).

MARION E. NEVILLE-LYNCH passed away in 2009. She was an Associate Professor of Literacy at Brooklyn College, The City University of New York, where she also served as Graduate Deputy and Program Head for the Graduate Literacy Program. She was the Literacy Coordinator for the Childhood Education Program and supervised teacher candidates in the New York public schools. Dr. Neville-Lynch received her doctorate in education from Teachers College, Columbia University. Her most recent publication was *Assessing Personal Beliefs and Values for Classroom Instruction.*

CHARISE PIMENTEL is an Assistant Professor in the Department of Curriculum & Instruction at Texas State University-San Marcos. She has a Ph.D. in the Foundations of Education from the University of Utah and she specializes in the areas of Race and Education, Bilingual Education, Multicultural Education, and Critical Whiteness Studies. Her research projects focus on examining the intersections of race and language and how these social constructs shape students' school experiences.

OCTAVIO PIMENTEL joined the Department of English at Texas State University San Marcos in 2005. He has taught various classes in composition, including first-year composition courses, advanced composition, technical writing, and various critical graduate courses that encompass issues of minority languages and writing. Critically trained in issues of rhetoric/writing and education, Dr. Pimentel combines both of these fields, while addressing critical issues of minoritized individuals in the composition field.

ELIZABETH QUINTERO has been involved with education programs in many states in the U.S. and several countries as teacher, research scholar, and curriculum specialist. Her focus is programs that serve young children and families in multilingual communities representing a variety of cultural and historical backgrounds. Through her work with Head Start programs, programs for English Language Learners, and bilingual family literacy programs, she uses critical theory, critical pedagogy, and critical literacy as effective for authentic participation, inclusion of multiple knowledge sources, and support for transformative action. She is a Professor of Education at California State University Channel Islands. Recent publications include: *Critical Literacy in Early Childhood Education: Artful Story and the Integrated Curriculum*. New York: Peter Lang.

LUPE RAMOS is a national board certified bilingual education teacher in the Austin Independent School District, as well as a National Association for Bilingual Education Teacher of the Year. She currently teaches in a dual language kindergarten classroom. She is a veteran teacher with 30 years of experience.

ALMA RUBAL-LOPEZ is a Professor at Brooklyn College, the City University of New York. She received her Ph.D. in bilingual developmental psychology from Yeshiva University. Dr. Rubal-Lopez is currently Program Head of Bilingual Education at Brooklyn College. She has authored numerous journal articles and co-authored *On Becoming Nuyoricans,* which takes an intimate look at two sisters' experiences growing up as part of the first generation of female Puerto Ricans born and raised in New York during the 1950s and 1960s. Dr. Rubal-Lopez also co-edited *Post-Imperial English: Status Change in Former British and American Colonies, 1940-1990*.

DELIDA SANCHEZ, Ph.D. is an Assistant Professor in School Counseling at Brooklyn College—City University of New York. She earned her Ph.D. in Counseling Psychology from Columbia University Teachers College. She's a National Institutes of Health grant recipient for her research on racism-related stress, health risk factors, and psychological outcomes among adolescents of color. Her professional interests include supervision, multicultural training, school counseling and consultation.

María del Rosario Scharrón-del Río was born and raised in Río Piedras, Puerto Rico. She is the eldest daughter of Rosario del Río Muñiz, an early childhood and elementary school educator, and Rafael Scharrón Alicea, a musician within the bolero (música de tríos) genre. She received her Ph.D. in Clinical Psychology from the University of Puerto Rico, Río Piedras. After completing her clinical internship at the Harvard Medical School in Boston, she worked as a child psychologist at the Washington Heights Family Health Center, a primary-care clinic that serves a predominantly Latino/a immigrant community in New York City. Currently she is an assistant professor at the School Counseling Program in Brooklyn College's School of Education, City University of New York (CUNY). She is an active advocate around diversity and inclusion issues within her immediate community (Brooklyn College, CUNY, and New York City) and within educational, counseling, and psychological settings. Her research focuses on ethnic and cultural minority psychology and education, including multicultural competencies, mental health disparities, spirituality, resiliency, and well-being.

Lourdes Diaz Soto is Full Professor and the Goizueta Endowed Chair at Dalton State College. Her research interest focuses on issues of social justice and equity especially regarding Latino/a children and families. She has published extensively including books, several edited volumes, numerous book chapters as well as scholarly pieces in peer-reviewed journals. Her recent publications include: Latino Education in the U.S .(Rowan & Littlefield Education); and an article with her graduate students Claudia Cervantes-Soon, Elizabeth Villareal and Emmet E. Campos in the *Harvard Educational Review* titled, Xicana Sacred Space: A Communal Circle of Compromiso for Educational Researchers. She is "grandmother,""abuelita," and "nana" to Jose, Juan, and Antonio Ponton as well as Maya Isabella Soto and Bruce David Soto.

Dr. Luis Urrieta, Jr. is Associate Professor of Cultural Studies in Education and Mexican American Studies at the University of Texas-Austin. Dr. Urrieta's research interests center around (1) cultural and racial identities, (2) agency as social and cultural practices, and (3) social movements related to education. He has been recognized as a fellow by the American Educational Research Association, the Spencer Foundation, the Lee Hage Jamail Regents Chair in Education (UT), and most recently by the U.S. Department of State Fulbright Commission (2009–2010). In 2009, Dr. Urrieta published *Working from Within: Chicana and Chicano Activist Educators in Whitestream Schools* with the University of Arizona Press. He has also published book chapters as well as several articles in peer-reviewed journals.

Index

Studies in the Postmodern Theory of Education

General Editors
Joe L. Kincheloe & Shirley R. Steinberg

Counterpoints publishes the most compelling and imaginative books being written in education today. Grounded on the theoretical advances in criticalism, feminism, and postmodernism in the last two decades of the twentieth century, Counterpoints engages the meaning of these innovations in various forms of educational expression. Committed to the proposition that theoretical literature should be accessible to a variety of audiences, the series insists that its authors avoid esoteric and jargonistic languages that transform educational scholarship into an elite discourse for the initiated. Scholarly work matters only to the degree it affects consciousness and practice at multiple sites. Counterpoints' editorial policy is based on these principles and the ability of scholars to break new ground, to open new conversations, to go where educators have never gone before.

For additional information about this series or for the submission of manuscripts, please contact:

Joe L. Kincheloe & Shirley R. Steinberg
c/o Peter Lang Publishing, Inc.
29 Broadway, 18th floor
New York, New York 10006

To order other books in this series, please contact our Customer Service Department:

(800) 770-LANG (within the U.S.)
(212) 647-7706 (outside the U.S.)
(212) 647-7707 FAX

Or browse online by series:
www.peterlang.com